D1285417

SALISBURY
AND THE MEDITERRANEAN

STUDIES IN POLITICAL HISTORY

Editor: Micheal Hurst
Fellow of St John's College, Oxford

SALISBURY
AND THE
MEDITERRANEAN
1886–1896

by

C. J. LOWE

LONDON: Routledge & Kegan Paul
TORONTO: University of Toronto Press
1965

First published 1965
in Great Britain by
Routledge & Kegan Paul Ltd
and in Canada by
University of Toronto Press

Printed in Great Britain by
W. & J. Mackay & Co Ltd

© *C. J. Lowe 1965*

No part of this book may be reproduced
in any form without permission from
the publisher, except for the quotation
of brief passages in criticism

To Gillian

CONTENTS

PREFACE

THE research upon which this book is based was begun in 1952 under the supervision of the late Sir Charles Webster and Miss Hilda Lee of the London School of Economics and continued under his successor, Professor W. N. Medlicott. I would like to take this opportunity of expressing the debt of gratitude that I owe them for much kindly assistance. My thanks are due also to Professor Mario Toscano for facilitating my access to certain files of the Italian Foreign Ministry archives, and to Dr. J. F. A. Mason for permitting me to use the Salisbury Papers. Mr. Michael Hurst of St. John's College, Oxford gave me the benefit of much helpful criticism, for which I am very grateful. Extended visits to Rome and Vienna were made possible, initially by the Rotary Foundation, more recently by sabbatical leave and financial assistance from the University of Durham: I hope they think it was worth it. Finally I should add that this book was written before the publication of Dr. Grenville's *Lord Salisbury and Foreign Policy*.

C. J. LOWE

Passfield Hall,
London, W.C.1

'Whatever government or whatever party may be in power, the English people are determined never to forfeit the maritime predominance in the Mediterranean . . . which cannot be shaken, as they well know, without imperilling the Empire.'

The Times, 14 October 1893.

I

THE DEFENCE
OF CONSTANTINOPLE

> Whatever happens will be for the worse and therefore it
> is our interest that as little should happen as possible.
>
> Salisbury in 1887.

THE major problems of foreign policy which faced Salisbury
when he became Prime Minister in August 1886 were in
the Mediterranean. British interest in this region, traditional
since the time of Pitt, lay in its importance as a means of communication with the Indian Empire and its value in this respect
had been enormously increased since the opening of the Suez
Canal in 1869. For England in the nineteenth century, maintenance of control of India was the paramount consideration,
since it was the key to British predominance in Asia. India was
the leading military station in the Empire providing free billets
for half the British Army, the source of an inexhaustible supply
of manpower and a useful export market. This much was
common to both parties for, whatever Gladstone thought about
Ireland, he never considered giving up India: certainly Dilke,
writing in 1887 on defence problems, took it as axiomatic that
India would be defended and, indeed, felt the need to argue
that other objects of concern even existed![1] Since Palmerston's
time it had been assumed that the vital British interest in the
Mediterranean was to maintain the independence of the Ottoman Empire and thus block the Russian drive on Constantinople. The Crimean War had been fought for this and as

---

[1] Dilke, *The Present Position of European Politics*, pp. 288 ff.; Robinson and
Gallacher, *Africa and the Victorians*, p. 13.

recently as 1878 the country had been on the brink of war with Russia for the same reason. The main object of British diplomacy at the Berlin Congress, an object which was successfully achieved, had been to keep Russia and her presumed satellite, Bulgaria, pinned back to the Balkan Mountains: and, not content with this, Disraeli and Salisbury had proceeded to bolster up the Sultan's dominions with the guarantee of his territories contained in the Cyprus Convention. Thus, so far, the main aim of foreign policy was clear: British interest in the maintenance of the Indian Empire demanded that Russia be kept out of Constantinople.

But, by 1886, the position had been complicated by two new factors. In the first place events in Bulgaria in 1885 had presented the powers with a *fait accompli*, wrecked the provisions of the Berlin Congress, and demonstrated that the assumption that Bulgaria would be a Russian satellite was false. Consequently by 1886 British policy had changed in this respect: the union of the two Bulgarias was recognised and it was now assumed that the best defence of Constantinople lay in assisting Bulgaria to maintain her independence of Russian control, rather than reverting to the Turkish control of Eastern Roumelia as provided for in 1878 which Russia now supported.

In the second place there was the British occupation of Egypt. When Salisbury had left office in 1880, England and France had been co-operating in the Dual Control: but Arabi Pasha's revolt and the refusal of France and Italy to participate in its suppression, had forced Gladstone to act alone. Once committed to this, what had originally been conceived of as a temporary expedient to relieve a dangerous situation, changed by imperceptible degrees into a determination to create stable government in Egypt; a relatively long term prospect. This, inevitably, gave rise to friction with France, complicated at the time by Bismarck's colonial campaign, and a certain amount of resentment on the part of the Sultan who, like the French, felt that he had been tricked out of Egypt. Since, owing to the complicated nature of Egyptian finances, the collaboration of the European powers was necessary for any effective schemes for reform, this created an increasingly delicate position, as Gladstone discovered in 1884–5. Either England submitted to Bismarck's 'Egyptian lever' or she faced the consequences of isolation, with all that this entailed for her interests in the Mediterranean and other parts of the world. The only alternative was evacuation, the solution which became increasingly attractive not only to Liberals like Harcourt, but also to Conservatives such as Salisbury.

Hence in August 1886 there were two main difficulties: how to support Bulgaria and thus keep Russia out of Constantinople; how to arrange Egyptian affairs so as to get rid of French hostility and the Egyptian lever, yet take account of the very real British interest in the security of the Suez Canal and the perils of isolation. The solution of these problems was made worse by the character of British internal politics. The elections of 1886 had been fought almost entirely on the issue of Home Rule, and Ireland completely dominated the political scene, all but excluding any consideration of foreign affairs. This struck quite forcibly the few people who gave any attention to these abstruse matters, as Dilke put it at the time:

> when we are thinking about Ireland, which is very commonly the case, we are apt to forget all else, and both our relations with foreign Powers and those with our dependencies drop into the background.[1]

But to make matters worse neither the Conservatives nor the Liberals had a clear majority. The issue of Home Rule had split the Liberal Party which, otherwise, in alliance with Parnell would have controlled the House of Commons. But the Liberal-Unionists, some seventy-eight in number, led by such contrasts as Hartington and Chamberlain, although opposed to Gladstone's Irish policy would not join the Conservatives and, for the life of this Parliament, continued to sit on the Opposition benches. Hartington, though offered the Leadership of the House, declined: to accept would break up his following and all hopes of an eventual reconstruction of the Liberal party on non-Gladstonian lines. Hence the best Salisbury could obtain in August 1886 was a promise of support from the outside, support which gave him a working majority but which made any positive moves, apart from Ireland, extremely difficult. As he was to remark later, resolute government outside Ireland was impossible.[2]

[1] Dilke, p. 282.
[2] Chilston, *Chief Whip*, pp. 83–86.

To the difficulties created by the hypnotic effect of Ireland must be added those inherent in the presence of Churchill in a commanding position in the Cabinet. Leader of the House and Chancellor of the Exchequer, friend of Chamberlain and champion of Tory Democracy, he had committed himself not only to a radical programme at home but also to a swingeing attack upon traditional foreign policy. To Churchill involvement in European politics was sheer stupidity: there was no point in defending Constantinople or in spending vast sums on armaments: these would only increase the danger of British involvement in a European war. As he told Salisbury in his letter of resignation in December,

> I am pledged up to the eyes to large reductions of expenditure, and I cannot change my mind on this matter. If the foreign policy of this country is conducted with skill and judgment, our present huge and increasing armaments are quite unnecessary, and the taxation which they involve perfectly unjustifiable.

This attitude on the part of the Chancellor of the Exchequer made the conduct of foreign policy difficult enough; but Randolph, in addition to making it clear to the Russians that in his view England had no interest in the Balkans, and despite his advocacy of peace, retrenchment and reform, also insisted on a policy of bluster with France. Never backward in speaking his mind on any occasion, he bluntly told an emissary of Freycinet in September that England would never leave Egypt and that negotiation was impossible, an attitude which he afterwards maintained in the Cabinet.[1]

It was against this background that Salisbury and Iddesleigh (nominal Foreign Minister until the Cabinet reshuffle in January 1887) tried to conduct British foreign policy. Salisbury's own ideas were in complete contrast to Churchill's. The apostle of High Toryism at home, opposed to any schemes of radical reform as likely to alienate the rank and file of the party—the classes—without really satisfying Randolph's clients—the masses—he carried this same outlook over into foreign affairs. Traditional policy had been to support the Sultan and he could see no good reason to make any change. To Salisbury foreign

[1] Churchill, *Lord Randolph Churchill*, II, pp. 157, 172–4, 235; Cecil, *Life of Robert, Marquis of Salisbury*, IV, p. 322.

policy was the most important facet of government and it attracted him precisely because it was not susceptible to sudden changes. He did not regard it, as Churchill appeared to, as something which could be twisted around at will to fit in with the latest political fashions. In any case, with his memory of 1878, he was by no means so sure that the abandonment of Constantinople would turn out to be as popular as Churchill assumed. Moreover, since even Churchill recognised—even emphasised—the overriding need to defend India, what was the point of giving up the only means of retaliation for Russian moves in the Herat region that Britain possessed? Ten years later, after the Armenian massacres, Salisbury in fact came round to accepting much the same basic policy—giving up Constantinople, sticking in Egypt—that Churchill advocated in 1886, but at this time he strongly disagreed with him:

> I do not wholly take your view about our attitude towards Russia. I consider the loss of Constantinople would be the ruin of our party and a heavy blow to the country: and therefore I am anxious to delay by all means Russia's advance to that goal.[1]

All Salisbury's instincts were against radical changes in policy—this was evident throughout his control of the Foreign Office: in foreign, as in home affairs, patient diplomacy was the answer, whether in relation to the French over Egypt or Austria and Russia in the Balkans.

What Salisbury wanted to do in the autumn of 1886 was to placate the French with fair words and hints of a phased withdrawal, whilst renewing the negotiations with the Sultan which had broken down in 1885. This, it seemed, was obvious commonsense if he were simultaneously to oppose Russia in the Balkans. This he proposed to do by collaborating with Austria in a policy of support for Prince Alexander of Bulgaria. Both proposals were turned down by the Cabinet: Churchill would not permit negotiations with France whilst the most he would allow in the Balkans was for England to push Austria and Germany into taking the lead: this was perfectly easy to achieve he maintained, 'if the foreign policy of this country is conducted with skill and judgment'.[2]

[1] Churchill, II, p. 161.
[2] Ibid., p. 235; Robinson and Gallacher, pp. 261–2.

Consequently, until Churchill made his fatal blunder in December and presented Salisbury with the opportunity to get rid of him, foreign policy was reduced to working within the limits that he prescribed, a far from enviable situation for Salisbury and Iddesleigh. For the simple fact was that neither Germany nor Austria had any enthusiasm for the role in which Randolph had cast them.

The apparent gravity of the situation in Bulgaria was due to the expectation current in London that a Russian invasion was imminent in order to suppress the widespread hostility to General Kaulbars and his mission. Kaulbars, nominally Russian Minister at Sofia, had in fact assumed the 'protectorship' of Bulgaria after the enforced abdication of Alexander and was currently occupied with persuading the Bulgarian Assembly at Tirnova to elect a Russian candidate for the throne. Since this was meeting with little success, St. Petersburg, wounded in its *amour propre* by this patent ingratitude, adopted the view that the Bulgarian people were being terrorised into this anti-Russian course by 'bandits', from whom they would have to be liberated. It was this prospect of 'liberation' which was so alarming to London and led them to attempt to mobilise the support of the powers signatory to the Treaty of Berlin.

But the difficulty was that, in view of Churchill's attitude, it was extremely difficult to state with any assurance just what British policy was. Iddesleigh attempted it in a confidential memorandum at the end of September which was intended to bolster up the confidence of Vienna, but the effect was not very encouraging. As he admitted, owing to party politics, the nature of the constitution and the importance of public opinion, it was difficult to predict in advance what British policy would be on hypothetical issues: all he could say was that for a clearly defined object such as the defence of Constantinople, 'England no doubt would fight'. Yet, on the strength of this, Austria and Germany were expected to take a decided stand over Bulgaria. Bismarck was frank, brutally so: he did not intend to stir a finger for Prince Alexander or the Bulgarians. As far as he was concerned Bulgaria and even Constantinople was a Russian sphere of interest in which he would not intervene; in which he would not even permit Austria to intervene; he could not recognise as invoking the *casus foederis* of the Dual Alliance any war arising from Bulgaria. He suggested, somewhat ironically, that if England wished to oppose Russia in the Balkans she should hire the Turks, for *'mit Geld lässt sich in der Türkei alles machen'*.[1]

With Bismarck's attitude so devastatingly plain Iddesleigh could not hope for much from Kálnoky, particularly since it was by no means clear from the British memorandum whether in fact they would fight for Bulgaria. Kálnoky had the advantage over London in that he had been assured that Russia would not, except in the last resort, invade Bulgaria, and consequently he did not intend to take any unnecessary risks. He made this fairly plain to Paget in an interview on 7 November: not being able to count on the support of Germany and being uncertain of the support of other powers he would decline to do anything which might possibly provoke war with Russia unless in the last extremity. He did not think that simply to protect the Bulgarian people from the rough usage of General Kaulbars it was worth plunging Europe into war. If Russia showed unmistakable intention of taking possession of Bulgaria with a view to permanent establishment in the Balkans and arriving at Constantinople, then indeed a new phase calling for the most energetic action of Europe would have arrived and it would be easy in a very short time for the powers interested in the maintenance of the Ottoman Empire to come to an understanding as to what was to be done. This was as far as he would go for the present particularly since, as long as Churchill was in the Cabinet in London, British policy could not be relied upon.[2]

Thus, despite his own desire to maintain traditional policy at Constantinople and to collaborate with Austria in checking Russian influence in the Balkans, Salisbury, so far, had met with little success. The combination of Bismarck's complete reserve and the impression created abroad by Churchill's attitude had defeated him: all that he could do by November was to play a waiting game, waiting until one or the other of his obstacles

---

[1] Conf. Memo. 29 September 1886, printed in Temperley and Penson, *Foundations of British Foreign Policy*, pp. 442–4; White to Salisbury 15 August 1886, S.P.; G.P., IV, No. 864; V, No. 1014.

[2] Paget to Iddlesleigh 7 November 1886, F.O., 7/1097, No. 416; Kálnoky to Széchényi 27 February 1887, S.A.W., Geheimakten Karton Rot, 1.461 Liasse XIV; Medlicott, *The Mediterranean Agreements of 1887* in *Slavonic Review*, 1926, p. 69.

were removed. By January 1887 this had been achieved. Churchill played into his hands by his threat of resignation and was taken up: Bismarck, entangled in his negotiations with Italy and Austria for the renewal of the Triple Alliance, was suddenly much more accommodating. The result was that Salisbury was now able to pursue the policy of his choice, an agreement with Austria and Italy for the defence of the *status quo* in the Eastern Mediterranean, coupled with negotiations to set a term to the British occupation of Egypt and thus satisfy France: in other words, a return to the Crimean policies which Churchill had so vigorously opposed.[1]

The sudden change of front on Bismarck's part which led to the Mediterranean Agreements of February and March 1887 and increasing collaboration between England and the Triple Alliance over the next five years was due, in the first instance, to Italian pressure. Yet, since most studies of these agreements have necessarily been based upon German sources, there has been a marked tendency to look upon them from either the viewpoint of Berlin or of Vienna, the effect of which is to present them as offshoots of the Triple Alliance. Whilst there is clearly some justification for this view—it might well be contended that the Mediterranean Agreements were the cement which held the Triple Alliance together—it is an exaggeration, a reflection of the era of diplomatic history dominated by *Die Grosse Politik*. London and Rome, Salisbury, Rosebery, Robilant and Crispi, were not automats manipulated by Achitopel in Berlin, whatever the latter may have thought: they had their own reasons for entering upon these negotiations. Foremost among these on the Italian side were their colonial ambitions, which may be summed up in one word, Tripoli. Since the French seizure of Tunis in 1881 Italian eyes had become fixed upon Tripoli as their heritage in the Mediterranean. To some extent this was simply the search for commercial expansion on the part of firms such as the Rubattino steamship company, or the Milanese interests behind the *Società di esplorazione commerciale*, which put up the funds for most of the Italian explorations of Africa in the 1880's. But, although it had, at least in part, been responsible

[1] Pribram, *The Secret Treaties of Austria-Hungary*, II, pp. 56 ff.; Langer, *European Alliances*, pp. 390–6; For the circumstances of Churchill's resignation see Churchill, II, pp. 232–40, and James, *Lord Randolph Churchill*, Ch. X.

for the original interest in colonial activities, the search for commercial markets never became the major element in Italian colonial expansion: in fact, after 1885, northern industrialists and the Milan newspaper *La Perseveranza* became its major opponents. This for reasons which were evident enough since the enormous expenditure involved, which they as taxpayers paid for, was out of all proportion to any benefit they derived through increased trade. In any case Italian industry was highly protected and insufficiently developed to feel any urgent need of foreign markets.

The pressure for colonial expansion in Italy came not from the industrial north but from the agrarian south. In part this was age old: landless Sicilian peasants made up the major part of the European population of Tunis in the 1870's. But by the mid-eighties the problem was more acute: the French had closed the door in Tunis whilst increasing agrarian distress in Italy was having a marked effect upon politics. Hence the almost complete unanimity with which southern politicians took up colonial expansion in 1884–5: mass emigration would alleviate the problems caused by over-population on the land without the necessity of touching the awkward problem of land reform. From 1884 onwards the *colonialisti* became a group in the Chamber whom ministers ignored at their peril, a pressure which grew correspondingly greater with the increasing distress in the south consequent upon the commercial tariff war with France.[1]

To this was added the conception of national prestige. Italian self-esteem had suffered a bitter blow by the French annexation of Tunis in 1881. Increasingly since 1870 the Mediterranean had been thought of, particularly on the Left—in power since 1876—as *mare nostrum*: with the recovery of Rome, they predicted, Italy would once more rise to Imperial grandeur. This idea, even if it did not make France the major enemy in place of Austria, certainly placed a strain upon the conception of *la sorella latina*, and provided one of the basic incentives for the German alliance. Resentment at French patronage of Italy since the days of Napoleon III, fears of French domination of the Mediterranean, of French intrigue via the 'Black International', determination to assert Italian strength to avoid

[1] Volpe, *Italia Moderna*, I, pp. 163–72, 182, 328; Carocci, *Agostino Depretis*, pp. 589–99; Ciasca, *Storia coloniale*, pp. 89–91.

further humiliation, were now added to the original, and continuing, anti-Austrian irredentism and gave a new direction to
Italian foreign policy. This was increasingly accepted now even
on the Right, the traditional exponents of a pro-French orienta-
tion since the days of Cavour. By 1884 diplomats such as Launay
or Robilant, alarmed lest further French expansion should go
unchecked, insisted on a stand against the major opponent in
the Mediterranean, since they feared that if France took
Morocco and Tripoli too the consequent popular explosion in
Italy would overthrow the monarchy, with all that this entailed.[1]

It was the combination of these pressures from Parliament
and from Italy's leading diplomats which induced leading
politicians, such as Mancini, previously opposed to colonial
ventures, to take a more direct interest in Tripoli in 1884. The
alarm in April, when it was feared that a French occupation of
Morocco was imminent, and in November, when it seemed that
the powers were about to carve up Africa between them, roused
public feeling in Italy and forced the Government to make a
stand. But the difficulty was that Bismarck, currently engaged
in his colonial campaigns against Gladstone, made it abundantly clear that he supported France, which meant that the
only possibility for action on Italy's part lay in joining in the
hunt with Bismarck and Ferry against England. Ferry in fact
suggested this as the basis of a Franco-Italian colonial *entente*.[2]

But for Mancini this was impossible. The Italian position in
Europe was somewhat peculiar. The Triple Alliance of 1882
had done very little to break down the basic hostility between
Berlin and Rome, still less between Vienna and Rome: all that
the treaty had accomplished from the Italian viewpoint was to
give them a breathing space during which they would be re-
lieved of the expectation of an Austrian crusade to liberate the
Papacy. The alliance had no application outside Europe, in
Africa Italy was left to fend for herself and Bismarck and Kálnoky repeatedly made it clear that if Italy became involved
with France through supporting England in Egypt, or through
opposing French moves in Tripolitania, then she would face the
consequences. In effect therefore, since there was no chance of

[1] Zaghi, *P. S. Mancini*, pp. 26, 69; Chabod, *Storia della politica estera*,
pp. 183, 294–305, 460–3, 477, 548.
[2] Zaghi, pp. 28–32, 46, 50–56.

a direct French attack upon Italy—the only contingency covered by the alliance—Italy gained no protection whatsoever for her Mediterranean interests from the alignment with Berlin. The solution to this situation advocated by Depretis, who had been extremely reluctant to make the alliance in the first place, was to improve relations with France, but not at the expense of relations with England. There was little to be gained in escaping the highly unpopular alliance with Vienna if it could only be achieved by making Italy dependent upon France: to join Bismarck and Ferry in 1884 would only make Rome dependent upon the whims of Paris in addition to those of Berlin. No Italian statesman could contemplate the alienation of England who, with good reason, was held to be 'the most sincere friend we have in Europe': this point had been expressly made in 1882 and received even greater emphasis in subsequent renewals of the alliance with the Central Powers.[1]

Hence Mancini avoided Ferry's overtures and instead, to Bismarck's wrath, initiated a campaign of collaboration with England at the Egyptian and Suez conferences, in the hope that out of this might come some solid Anglo-Italian understanding which would protect Italian interests in the Mediterranean. At the same time, in the expectation that some French *coup* in Morocco was imminent, he secretly prepared an expeditionary force with which to seize Tripoli as the Italian counterstroke. But, since Ferry's *coup* failed to materialise—partly owing to the growing French involvement in Indo-China—by the end of the year Mancini was left with an expeditionary force on his hands, since he hardly dared to precipitate a Mediterranean crisis by himself. It was one thing to take Tripoli as a reply to a French action in Morocco, quite another to bring the wrath of both London and Berlin upon himself alone. Instead Mancini now allowed himself to be diverted into the Massowa expedition which occupied Italian attention throughout 1885. This had the virtue of initiating collaboration with England in Africa but it failed to bring the wider results that Mancini hoped for—a Mediterranean alliance—and left the acquisition of Tripoli as far away as ever.[2]

[1] Catalani to Robilant 26 September 1886, A.M.E., s.p. 29/1368; Salvemini, *Politica Estera*, pp. 60–63, 73; Pribram, II, pp. 35–38.

[2] Salvemini, pp. 63–69; Zaghi, pp. 31–38, 51–56, 66–67, 72–76.

Hence the problem in 1886 was still that of 1884, the only difference being that Bismarck's colonial *entente* with France appeared to have broken down, whilst the tension in the Balkans suggested that Italy could now set a higher value upon herself as an alliance partner. Hence it ought to be possible, it seemed to Robilant, to both stick out for some guarantee of Italian Mediterranean interests against France from Germany and develop the association with England. But there was one danger in this: Bismarck might equally solve his problems by supporting Russian views in the Balkans, in which case an understanding with England, unless it were strictly confined to opposing France, would lead to considerable embarrassment. Hence until it was clear which way Bismarck was going to jump Italian policy had to remain flexible: Robilant was sure enough of his ground to insist on German support over Tripoli as the price of renewal of the alliance, but whether this should be envisaged in collaboration with England or with France depended upon Bismarck. Hence the tentative nature of the soundings at London in September for a Mediterranean alliance, and the insistence that it should apply only to the Mediterranean and not to the Balkans: hence too the immediate relay of Freycinet's overtures for a Franco-Italian alliance directed against England to Berlin, since this provided the ideal lever with which to force Bismarck to take sides. Bismarck's reply on 17 October decided the issue:

> Quand il s'agirait pour l'Italie de choisir entre la France et l'Angleterre pour les questions de la Mediterranée, S. (on) A. (ltesse) pense que de ces deux puissances l'Angleterre serait l'Allié la moins dangereuse pour l'Italie . . . il n'hésite pas à formuler son opinion dans ce sens qu'il serait tout contraire tout à l'interêt de l'Allemagne qu'à celui de l'Italie d' (entrer) dans les vues de la France.[1]

With this clear declaration of intent from Bismarck, Robilant now set about obtaining his alliance with England. On 22 October he sent for Lumley and told him that he was ready to discuss the Egyptian question, a suggestion that he repeated at

[1] Launay to Robilant 17 October 1886, A.M.E., *Carte Robilant*, 28; Robilant to Launay 5 August, to Nigra 2 October, 15 November 1886, A.M.E., *Gabinetto*, T.A. cass. lb.; Iddlesleigh to Salisbury 25, 27 September 1886, S.P.

intervals throughout November, culminating in a public speech emphasising Anglo-Italian solidarity in the Mediterranean. When, rather to his annoyance, this failed to bring the overtures from England that he expected, at last at the end of December, on instructions from Berlin, he took the bull by the horns and opened negotiations in London, reluctantly abandoning the advantage he had hoped to gain by pushing London into making the first move. Corti saw Salisbury on 7 and 17 January, called attention to Robilant's speech of 28 November, and suggested that the time had come for an Anglo-Italian understanding:

> The Italian government thought that, while persevering in the endeavour to maintain peace, it would nevertheless be advisable while there was still time to prepare the way for eventual action on the part of England and Italy, with a view to the protection of their common interests especially in the Mediterranean and its neighbourhood. Both Powers would thus be prepared to enter into special arrangements under certain circumstances whenever the urgency of the case . . . (demanded) . . . The nature and form of the common action might be reserved as the subject of subsequent negotiations to be commenced whenever circumstances rendered it necessary. . . . In every eventuality the Italian Govt. were firmly determined to uphold their interests by such measures as circumstances might call for and those interests could in no case be antagonistic to those of Great Britain.[1]

Salisbury's reply reflected his current preoccupations. The Italian approaches in September and October had left him and Iddesleigh unmoved because they were directed to the wrong quarter. What they wanted was support in Bulgaria, which Robilant was unwilling to give; what they were offered, support in Egypt, was of dubious value. There was little advantage to be gained by this since Robilant's *quid pro quo*—the cession of Zeila —would infuriate the Sultan, whilst if Salisbury were going to attempt an Egyptian settlement he needed at least the benevolence of France. This was incompatible with a Mediterranean alliance with Italy as Robilant fully realised. It is in fact probable that one of the major aims of his advances had been to nip

[1] Robilant to Catalani 22 October 1886, A.M.E., s.p. 29/1368; to Corti 9 December 1886, A.M.E., Tel. 113/1013; Lumley to Iddesleigh 5, 18, 28 November 1886, F.O., 45/550, Nos. 301, 330, 349.

such an understanding in the bud.[1] But now, in January, it seemed that Italy might be offering support in Bulgaria after all. Corti's original suggestions were a bit vague on this score but that Salisbury assumed he was referring to the Eastern Mediterranean seems evident. In his reply to Corti requesting a closer definition of the Italian proposals he spoke of the legitimacy of Italian interests 'in the Black Sea, in the Aegean, in the Adriatic or on the coast of Africa'; to Morier, in St. Petersburg, he wrote as though the recruitment of Italy to the defence of the *status quo* in the East was an accomplished fact:

> Nor will Austria want for other allies. Italy is very deeply pre-occupied with the menace which any disturbance of the European peace in S.E. Europe might carry with it to Italian interests on the shore of the Mediterranean and she has made overtures to us very unusual in the earnestness . . . with which they are pressed.[2]

Hence Robilant's detailed proposals when they arrived on 1 February were something of a surprise. Although the covering letter spoke of 'the paralysing effect his proposals would have upon Russian menaces', their effect seemed to be 'to offer an alliance in case of war against France'. This Salisbury would not accept: as he pointed out to Corti, if he were to commit himself in advance against France then Robilant's successor might start a war for the recovery of Nice and Savoy. But, provided that this aspect were removed, there were no objections to an understanding. Tripoli itself presented no problem, even at this stage Salisbury assured Corti that 'if circumstances arise for it, Tripoli should be occupied by Italy and not by France'. This involved little or no commitment against France since it was highly unlikely that the French would move against Tripoli anyway: and, as Corti[3] assured him, it was not that Italy had any intention of

[1] British negotiations with France over Egypt alarmed Robilant: to Corti 9 December 1886, A.M.E., Tel. 113, No. 1013. On Bulgaria he took the line that the Russian interest was fully justifiable: to Catalani 8 October 1886, A.M.E., s.p. 29/1368.

[2] Salisbury to Morier 19 January 1887, S.P.; Salisbury to Lumley 17 January 1887, F.O., 45/572, No. 10A; G.P., IV, No. 887.

[3] Ibid.; Corti to Robilant 1, 6 February 1887, A.M.E., *Gabinetto*, cass. 6; Salisbury to the Queen 24 January, 1 February 1887, *Letters*, I, pp. 261–70; Cecil, IV, pp. 15–20.

attacking France but simply that they wished for an insurance against a repetition of the Tunis affair. If these were also Robilant's views, and he confirmed this on 7 February, there were considerable advantages to be gained from an agreement with Italy linking England with the Central Powers. Salisbury's great fear at this time was that Bismarck's sabre-rattling in the Reichstag meant that a Franco-German war was imminent: Hatzfeldt had told him on 24 January that Germany would have to attack France immediately if Boulanger's warlike preparations continued. If this occurred it was only too likely that, as Hatzfeldt suggested, Russia would take the opportunity to impose her own Balkan settlement with the probability of an attack on Austria. If this happened England, obsessed with Ireland, would be hard put to defend her interests in south-east Europe, whilst any intervention in the West would be out of the question, despite the obligation to defend Belgium. But with an Anglo-Italian agreement to work together in the East, blessed by Bismarck, the situation would be very different. Austria would now feel secure enough to make a stand and, with any luck, Russia would be so impressed by this coalition that she would not move anyway.[1]

Thus it was already clear by 1 February that there was a large amount of agreement between Robilant and Salisbury, the only differences being over the somewhat startling Article IV, and there is every reason to suppose that they would have arrived at an agreement eventually in any case. But Bismarck was in a hurry. After considerable last-minute difficulties with Kálnoky he had at last got his agreement to the revised treaty of the Triple Alliance: now it was essential to speed up Robilant's negotiations so that the Anglo-Italian agreement and revised alliance could be signed quickly before Kálnoky had any more last-minute misgivings. That Bismarck was primarily concerned with the East and not the West in these Anglo-Italian negotiations emerged quite clearly at this time. No doubt if Salisbury would also assume the obligations envisaged in Robilant's first draft against France this would be all to the good, but it was not the essential point. The real object of interest to Bismarck was to commit Salisbury in the East, thus

[1] Salisbury to Morier 19 January 1887, S.P.; to the Queen 24 January 1887, *Letters*, I, pp. 261 ff.

at the same time making sure that Italy honoured her obligations—of which Vienna was doubtful—and ensuring for himself
much greater freedom of manoeuvre in his relations with Russia.
Hence his assurances to Malet on 1 February that there was no
need for any agreement directed against France, 'an understanding concerning the East was all that was necessary',
coupled with dire hints of what would follow if Salisbury rejected the Italian advances:

> . . . the Powers interested would have to seek other combina-
> tions. He could, for instance, easily patch up matters with
> France by yielding to her constant solicitations concerning
> Egypt. He could ward off all apprehension from Russia by
> reducing his alliance with Austria to its literal engagement to
> maintain the integrity of the Austrian Empire and allowing
> Russia to take not Constantinople but the Bosphorous and the
> Dardanelles.[1]

This decided the Cabinet. With Churchill gone there was no
opposition to Salisbury's views and on 2 February they autho-
rised him to reply with an acceptance of Robilant's draft
provided that Article IV were excluded, whilst Hatzfeldt was
now persuaded to give a guarantee of German support in Egypt
as an additional inducement. The only possible obstacle was
now Robilant and the extent to which he would insist on the
anti-French aspects of the agreement. In fact he made no difficulty about this. He certainly had no intention of attacking
France: as he told Salisbury later, a strong France was an
essential part of the European balance upon which Italy, as the
weakest power, depended. Such a war was in his view 'an
improbable event': all he wanted was to make sure that no
possible European combination could give France Tripoli since
this would raise such a storm in Italy that it might produce a
war. Moreover, on 5 February the Government in which
Robilant was Foreign Minister resigned and the essential now
became to obtain what Salisbury would willingly give with all
possible speed before Italian domestic politics ruined his
chances. Hence the rapidity of his revised draft, given to Salisbury on 9 February, presented to and adopted by the Cabinet

[1] Malet to Salisbury 1 February 1887, F.O., 64/1155, No. 33; G.P., IV,
Nos. 841, 885, 887, 893; H.P., III, pp. 194–204.

the next day, and the willingness to accept even Salisbury's suggestion of an exchange of notes rather than a convention, a method which would enable him to deny to Parliament that he had signed anything. After all, Salisbury had already told him that such an understanding 'would have the same effect for England as if they were to make a treaty'.[1]

Hence by February 1887 Salisbury had at last obtained what he had been after since the summer of 1886, an agreement which linked the Central Powers to the defence of the *status quo* in the East, an agreement which was now enhanced by the adherence of Austria. The main reasons for Kálnoky's reluctance in the past had been the attitude of Berlin and the unreliability of British policy influenced by Churchill: now, with Berlin pressing him from 16 February onwards to join the Anglo-Italian coalition, and with Churchill gone, he was persuaded to open negotiations on 23 February for an agreement along the same lines as that between England and Italy. As emerged in the course of the discussions at London, Kálnoky, like Robilant, would have preferred a hard and fast alliance binding, 'not only the present but future British governments'. But Salisbury demurred to this. An agreement with Italy was a relatively safe political move in view of their traditional friendship: as he had told Corti before, 'there was no nation with whom common action would be more agreeable to the people of this country than with Italy'. But even in this case Salisbury had felt it unsafe to risk his parliamentary position by signing a treaty. Although convinced himself that British interests would demand that they support Austria in the event of war, he thought it very doubtful if this equally applied to Gladstone, whose views on the subject of Austria and Turkey were notorious. But in the course of these discussions he said enough to convince Kálnoky that a political agreement was worthwhile, leaving the military decisions to be dictated by the course of events, and these limitations were distinctly recognised in a letter to Salisbury of 12 March which was to form the basis of the British Note:

[1] Robilant to Corti 26 January, Corti to Robilant 1, 6, 9 February 1887, A.M.E., Cassetta Verde, n. 6, fasc. 1; Salisbury to the Queen 2 February 1887, *Letters*, I, p. 269; G.P., IV, Nos. 886–92. Robilant's draft of 26 January (given to Salisbury on 1 February) is printed in G.P., IV, No. 887. The notes as exchanged on 12 February are in Pribram, I, pp. 95–96.

In the first place he recognised again distinctly that, whatsoever the future might bring, the proposed interchange of notes was not a promise of material support on either side, but was a definition of policy on the part of the two Powers acting in harmony to be pursued by moral and diplomatic means. In the second place he called my attention to the circumstances that the interests of Austria were not engaged in the western basin of the Mediterranean but were confined to the Aegean and the Exine. At the same time H.E. took care to note that though Austria's special interests in the Egyptian Question were not large she would heartily support the policy of H.M.G. in regard to Egypt.[1]

Nevertheless, this arrangement held considerable advantages for Austria. Apart from the clearer definition of British policy, by this means—adherence to the agreements of 12 February—Austria had obtained what Robilant had rejected in the renewal of the Triple Alliance, certainty of Italian support in the East. In this way England had now become the cement which held the Triple Alliance together, a fact which explains the considerable attention that Kálnoky afterwards paid to the maintenance of these agreements in which he had not, originally, been a participant, or even shown much interest.

Thus far then, by the end of March, Salisbury had committed England to a general political understanding with Italy and Austria in the Mediterranean, leaving specific arrangements for co-operation to be made as and when the need arose. His next move was to try to use this situation—the absence of Churchill and the support of Bismarck—to revive the idea of a negotiated withdrawal from Egypt, and for this purpose Drummond-Wolff was now sent back to Constantinople. Bismarck, as far as can be discerned, honoured his commitment—for which he extracted further payment in Zanzibar—for White had no complaints and the French were quite impressed with Radowitz's support of the British proposals. But Russian and French opposition killed the project. The logic of the Russian opposition was clear enough: only Egypt kept Britain and France apart. That of France was less decided. After all, Freycinet had been the main advocate of an Egyptian settlement in the previous autumn and,

[1] Salisbury to Paget 16 March 1887, F.O., 7/1114, No. 52; G.P., IV, Nos. 893–8; Medlicott, p. 74; Temperley and Penson, p. 447. Texts in B.D., VIII, pp. 6–8.

although he disliked Salisbury's insistence on the right of re-entry, the conclusion of the agreement would at least offer some prospect of getting the British out. Hence his initial hesitation to oppose and, although Russian pressure may have been a contributory factor, it seems likely that he only came to his final decision as a result of the Boulangist crisis in May. Getting rid of Boulanger was difficult enough without making Rochefort a present in the form of Egypt.

The failure of the Drummond-Wolff negotiations in this manner had a marked effect beyond that of the obvious continuance of the British presence in Egypt. Not so much upon Salisbury since, although in July he could talk of the 'silver lining even to the great black cloud of a Franco-German war', it was by no means clear that the French had not rendered him a service: White, for one, advocated offering the French Ambassador the Order of the Bath for his work. Certainly, after this, it would be difficult for the French to raise the Egyptian question again, and there is no reason to suppose that Anglo-French relations were any worse after this event. By October there had been a string of colonial agreements, including the vexed question of the Suez Canal, and Salisbury was as opposed as ever to anything which might unleash another Franco-German war. Similarly with Russia, although Salisbury rejected Giers advances for an Anglo-Russian understanding on the Balkans—probably because it would wreck his recent agreements with the Triple Alliance—he equally rejected Italian schemes for recognition of Coburg as Prince of Bulgaria and naval demonstrations in the Black Sea. Hence, although it is true that it was the failure of the Drummond-Wolff negotiations which initiated the moves which led to the second stage of the Mediterranean Agreements at the end of 1887, this was not due to Salisbury, who was not unduly perturbed by the events of the summer. British preoccupation with the menace of the Franco-Russian bloc in the Mediterranean came as the result of the naval scare of 1888: the first to be afflicted, in July 1887, was not Salisbury but Crispi and Kálnoky.[1]

[1] Salisbury to Kennedy 19, 25 August 1887, F.O., 45/577, Tel. 71;/573, No. 254; Cecil, IV, pp. 48–53, 65–67; G.P., IV, Nos. 907–10; V, Nos. 909–13; de Staal, I, pp. 351–8; Smith, *Embassy of Sir William White*, pp. 75–91. D.D.F., VI, Nos. 535, 559.

The idea that the Mediterranean Agreements should be extended to include Turkey as a participant member had been advocated in Berlin in February and March, largely as a means of distracting the Sultan from his current application to join the Triple Alliance. At the time it was not taken very seriously: Kálnoky suggested that he should first compose his differences with England over Egypt before this could be considered. But the idea was revived in July by the Italians as a means of combating the growing Franco-Russian influence at Constantinople, and gained force when it received Austrian support in August. Crispi, who finally replaced Depretis at the end of July, was, with Blanc, now Ambassador at Constantinople, the main instigator of this scheme. Robilant and Depretis had always tried to keep out of the Bulgarian *imbroglio*, in which they could not see any direct Italian interest, but Crispi regarded it as a question of supporting Mazzinian principles and urged his allies to recognise Ferdinand of Coburg 'as a national demonstration of the wishes of the Bulgarian people'. Assuming that Russia was bound to intervene and that a general war would break out—a war which he thought would be as much to Italy's advantage as the Crimean had been—he thought it a matter of urgency that the allies should make sure of Turkey. Consequently Blanc now drew up a short memorandum which he gave to the Grand Vizier,

> with a view to enlist the sympathies of the Porte in favour of a community of action by the Mediterranean Powers in such a way as to reassure the Sultan as to any dangers he might run from France, even if supported by Russia.[1]

Austrian support for Crispi's schemes was the product of Kálnoky's increasing alarm at the drift of German policy at Constantinople following Bismarck's Re-insurance Treaty. In the spring, as Salisbury had noted, Radowitz had been at least neutral and even gave Drummond-Wolff his support but, in July, he openly campaigned for the Russian candidate in Bulgaria, from which Kálnoky drew the obvious conclusion. Hence the more power that could be infused into the Mediterranean

[1] Nigra to Depretis 18 April 1887, A.M.E., Cassetta Verde, Accessione Turchia, n. 231, fasc. 2; White to Salisbury 16 July 1887, S.P.; D.D.F., VI, bis. No. 49; Crispi, *Politica Estera*, pp. 144–54.

alliance the better it would be. Discussions began on 23 August between Calice and Blanc, with White hovering in the background, on the old suggestion of a tripartite agreement for the support of Turkey; discussions which were carried on throughout September until agreement was reached on 14 October. Kálnoky's object in these negotiations was 'to give Turkey moral courage for resistance to Russia', so that in the event of war the Turkish Army could be relied upon to fight. Obviously British support at Constantinople would do much to achieve this, but Kálnoky was reluctant to put any pressure on London at this stage, contenting himself with informing Paget of his aims whilst concentrating on agreeing terms with the Italians. Premature pressure at London, he feared, might defeat its own ends.[1]

Whilst Calice and Blanc were still engaged in discussion preliminary soundings were taken at Berlin through Crispi's visit to Bismarck at the end of September. The result was not at first very conclusive since, although there was every encouragement to Austria and Italy to proceed with their policy of bolstering up the Sultan, there was no indication of open German support. It was not until 22 October that Bismarck could be induced to promise that he would certainly keep the French quiet in case of a Balkan war and, in the meantime, to use his good offices at London to drag Salisbury into the scheme. Significantly as soon as this promise was given Kálnoky took action: on 25 October Biegeleben, the Austrian Chargé, communicated the proposed bases of agreement to Salisbury, extolling the wonderful opportunity this offered to enlist Bismarck's support; simultaneously Herbert Bismarck urged upon Malet the great chance this presented to pin down Crispi.

Neither suggestion made much impression upon Salisbury, who was inclined to suspect that the whole idea was an elaborate conception of Bismarck's to take the strain off his eastern frontier.

> If he can get up a nice little fight between Russia and the three Powers, he will have leisure to make France a harmless neighbour for some time to come. It goes against me to be one of the Powers in that unscrupulous game.

[1] Paget to Salisbury 8, 15 September, White to Salisbury 7 November 1887, S.P.; Medlicott, pp. 76–79.

In so far as the scheme had originated with Crispi he thought it one of the Italian premier's hare-brained ideas for controlling the Sultan, which would produce 'a close Russo-Turkish alliance within a week'; the result of his 'longing for some splashy interference in Bulgarian affairs'. Apart from these major drawbacks, in Salisbury's eyes the whole scheme was vitiated by its uselessness in 'building upon the Sultan's fitful and feeble disposition'.[1]

If this was Salisbury's attitude why, nevertheless, did the proposed agreement go through? Because, as he pointed out to the Queen long before he consulted his colleagues, adhesion was the lesser of two evils. Kálnoky in his covering letter and Bismarck in his talks with Malet, made it abundantly clear that if Salisbury were to reject the Austrian proposals it was very probable that Austria would have to seek a settlement with Russia. In some ways of course such a settlement would have been welcomed by Salisbury, but it brought with it the dreaded spectre of the alliance of the three Northern Courts, which had proved in the past so inimical to British interests. The agreements with Italy and Austria in the spring had offered some guarantee against this old bugbear and, as Salisbury had shown in July, it was worth some trouble to keep it in being. Consequently, if the Austrian price was the extension of the agreement to provide for the specific defence of Turkey in Bulgaria, then it was Salisbury's view that the Austrian proposals would have to be accepted, at least in outline. After all, there was a considerable chance that his fears of Bismarck's intentions might turn out to be imaginary.[2]

But the problem was, even if Salisbury was half converted, to extend this conviction to his Cabinet colleagues. The eight bases were put to them at a meeting on 3 November and the reaction, as far as it can be discerned, whilst not unfavourable in principle, was to seek further clarification of Austrian and German views. In particular the Cabinet were eager to extend the principle of the protection of Bulgaria, to a guarantee of Turkey in Asia, where much more direct British interests were involved. Secondly the suggestion that the agreement, when concluded, should be revealed to the Sultan, they thought dangerous. But with modifications of the text Salisbury thought the Cabinet

[1] Cecil, IV, pp. 70–71.
[2] Ibid.; Medlicott, p. 82.

would accept the proposals, though a definite decision was to be postponed until 11 November. In the meantime Salisbury sought some clarification of German views, in particular some assurance that her new-found enthusiasm for opposing Russia would last a change of ruler.

This assurance Bismarck was perfectly willing to give since, as Kálnoky had already pointed out, the reliability of any Austro-Italian agreement—such as the proposal under consideration—depended entirely upon whether or not England should adhere to it. Without this adhesion, despite Crispi's fair words and ready promises, Austria could not safely embark upon a war with Russia in the Balkans. Not that Bismarck envisaged this agreement as a preliminary to war; this was precisely the time of his clash with the Army on this issue; rather it gave him a freer hand *vis-à-vis* Russia in that it enabled Austria to stand on her own feet. Hence his ready acceptance of the suggestion that he should communicate the essence of the Dual Alliance to Salisbury and Goschen, and the private letter which he wrote for communication to the Cabinet in general on 22 November, a letter in which he stressed that support for Austria was a necessity for Germany. The key figure in the Cabinet was Goschen, the Chancellor of the Exchequer, and his persuasion, after Bismarck's confidences, swayed the issue. But on one point Goschen was adamant; he could not consent to the Sultan being made privy to the treaty, as Vienna and Rome suggested, nor would he allow any inspired leakage in order to warn off the Russians. As he explained to Hatzfeldt, any hint of this agreement in the Press would raise a public storm in England, in which he would be fatally compromised. It was this fact, strongly supported by Salisbury, which determined both Article 9 of the eventual text and the form of the agreement, an exchange of notes. This, thought Salisbury, would cause him less embarrassment in Parliament; a wise precaution in view of later events.[1]

The draft British reply was sent to Rome and Vienna on 25 November and on 5 December Kálnoky, after concerting with Nigra, sent a final Austro-Italian draft to London as the basis for their identic note. This was accepted in its entirety and on 12 December the exchange of notes took place. This time, in

[1] G.P., IV, Nos. 920–4, 929–37.

contrast with those exchanges earlier in the year, the British Note was much more specific. Kálnoky's 9 Points were literally translated word for word and written into the English text. The only difference between the notes lay in the preamble and here it is noticeable that, whereas Kálnoky took his stand on the *entente* of the previous March, Salisbury glossed this over and took as the basis of agreement the Treaty of Berlin; a fairly obvious precaution against internal criticism and a reflection of his view that these were no new treaty obligations.[1]

What did this second exchange of notes achieve? Salisbury was inclined to be sceptical. This exchange of notes was less binding upon the British Government than their obligations under the Treaties of Paris and Berlin and, as he pointed out to White,

> If an emergency should arise during the tenure of a Minister or a Parliament disposed to recognise the obligations of Paris and Berlin, the understanding to which we have just come with Austria and Italy will not be needed to make him act.

On the whole Salisbury was rather puzzled by the keenness of German and Austrian interest. This was much simpler than Salisbury suspected. The March agreements had been signed by Robilant, those of December by Crispi. The Sicilian was an object of considerable distrust in Vienna and Berlin and the suggestion that this agreement would keep Crispi 'dans la bonne voie' meant literally what it said; and, as Bismarck continually pointed out, English cement was needed to this purpose. Kálnoky had also another object in view. Apart from keeping Crispi up to the mark, his original intention was to use the agreement to browbeat the Sultan. The Franco-Russian bloc alarmed him and, as he told Salisbury, this was the ideal moment to reverse their influence since now, in October, they could rely on German support at Constantinople when presenting their agreement to the Sultan virtually as an ultimatum. This idea was of course wrecked by Goschen and Salisbury's opposition to publication and hence the agreement for Kálnoky lost some of its value. Whether it would have achieved its purpose even if carried out as planned is doubtful but certainly

---

[1] British draft of 25 November and final texts in B.D., VIII, pp. 11–15; Kálnoky's draft of 5 December in G.P., IV, No. 938, Anlage I.

in the next few years Russo-French influence continued unabated.

For Crispi the main object in the negotiations had been to control the Sultan. Here he wanted to go much farther, even, than Kálnoky and tried to write into the agreement some prior division of the Turkish Empire—a favourite scheme of his and Blanc's in these years. This idea was rejected by Kálnoky before the scheme was sent to London, so Salisbury did not have to squash it as he undoubtedly would have done. But, even though his more ambitious ideas were rejected, Crispi still thought it important to carry the more limited agreement through: 'the principal thing is to bring the negotiation to an end, so that Salisbury does not escape us'. Making certain of this became his main preoccupation over the next four years.[1]

[1] Cecil, IV, pp. 70–78; G.P., IV, No. 921, Anlage I and II; Crispi, *Politica Estera*, pp. 175–6; Temperley and Penson, p. 458.

II

QUADRUPLE ALLIANCE
OR TWO POWER STANDARD?

At first we were very cordial with Italy—which is our normal policy. But as Crispi's character developed we came to the conclusion that it was better to give him a wide berth.   Salisbury, December 1888.

As far as Salisbury was concerned the main object of the 1887 agreements had been the defence of the existing position in the Balkans and at Constantinople. By the spring of 1888 this was virtually achieved when the Tsar, perhaps through knowledge of the Mediterranean League, tacitly accepted the position in Bulgaria, an attitude which took much of the tension out of Balkan politics and converted Anglo-Russian rivalry into a covert struggle for influence at the Porte, thus removing most of the dangers of war.[1] Instead now, for the next two years, most of the tension in the Mediterranean was focused at its western end with the alarming deterioration of Franco-Italian relations and a series of incidents which threatened several times to produce a war.

From the British point of view this was only slightly less alarming than the struggle in the eastern half which had dominated 1887 since, under the agreement of February 1887, there was some obligation to Italy if it should come to a French attack. The exact nature of this obligation was, however, still obscure. The Italians affected to regard it as a military alliance, which it certainly was not: Salisbury tended to dismiss the idea that he was under any obligation whatsoever, which he certainly

[1] Medlicott, pp. 87–88.

26

was. In a sense it can be said that this was the whole point of the diplomatic manoeuvring between London, Rome and Berlin in 1888: Salisbury wished to retain the Italian connection without being pushed into an alliance, Crispi and Bismarck wanted to exploit the apparently increasing danger from France to develop the 1887 understanding into a firm commitment. Hence the series of scares, often originated by Berlin, by which the Italians were persuaded to approach London for assistance: hence also, when these approaches failed to bring the desired result, Bismarck's own alliance offer to Salisbury in January 1889. But it does not follow from this, as Salvemini suggests, that Crispi was simply Bismarck's *agent provocateur*: this is to accept current French suspicions at their face value. In the first place there is no real evidence that Bismarck wanted to promote a war in 1888: in fact what evidence there is suggests the contrary, notably the Tunis schools affair in September–October. Secondly, this is to completely underestimate Crispi who was quite capable of creating diplomatic incidents without any prompting from Berlin.

Although French ministers, notably Goblet, were often highhanded in their attitude towards Italy in these years, there can be little doubt that the prime responsibility for the series of Franco-Italian incidents in 1888 lay with Crispi. French ministers and diplomats at the time and French historians since assumed that the object of his policy was to provoke a war with France, a war which by virtue of the Triple Alliance Italy was bound to win.[1] Whilst there is a certain amount of evidence to support this conclusion, notably Crispi's eagerness to negotiate a Military Convention with Berlin in 1887–8, on the whole a more charitable explanation of his Gallophobic crusade would seem nearer the truth. In the first place there was the tariff war, a conflict which, it must be stressed, Crispi inherited from his predecessor and which he did not create himself. This Franco-Italian commercial vendetta, which had important political consequences, originated less with Crispi than with the rising wave of protectionism in both the Italian and French Chambers. This had led in December 1886 to the Italian denunciation of

[1] De Moüy, *Souvenirs*, pp. 248 ff.; Goblet, *Souvenirs* in *Revue Politique et Parlementaire*, January, February 1929; Bourguin, *Les Politiques d'expansion imperialistes*, p. 128; D.D.F., VII, Nos. 41, 225, 245.

the Treaty of Commerce of 1881 with France, a treaty due to expire at the end of 1887, and the stipulation that it should be replaced by a treaty more advantageous to Italian interests. During the summer of 1887 Crispi had made strenuous efforts to achieve this, but with no success since, with the French Chamber similarly bent on improving the French commercial position, the Government in Paris could make no concessions to Italy and were increasingly doubtful if they could even now get a renewal of the 1881 agreement through the French Chamber. This is not to say that Crispi's handling of these negotiations was blameless. To say the least it was tactless of him to embark on his flamboyant visit to Prince Bismarck at Friedrichsruhe in the autumn of 1887 while these negotiations were in full swing: but the suggestion that this visit ruined what were otherwise very promising results is probably misplaced as Luzzatti, the leading delegate at Paris, was extremely doubtful if any results could be achieved in any case. All that can be said is that this visit and Crispi's parliamentary speeches on his return, with his reference to the measures which he was taking to prevent the Mediterranean from becoming a French lake, finally killed whatever desire there may have been in Paris to make concessions to Italian commercial demands, with the result that by the end of the year the Franco-Italian commercial Treaty had expired and a tariff war ensued.[1]

This war had disastrous consequences in Italy. France had been taking some thirty per cent. of Italian exports which were now drastically reduced. The situation was particularly acute for the wine producers of southern Italy whose export market almost completely disappeared; even more spectacular was the effect upon Italian credit of the widespread withdrawal of French money, as the French were the principal investors in Italian securities. The consequence of this was a rising wave of criticism of the Government particularly from the southern deputies whose constituencies were most affected by the commercial crisis and who were normally Crispi's closest supporters; increasingly this developed into a general onslaught upon his parliamentary position which he only survived after a series

[1] Crispi, *Politica Estera*, pp. 177–8, 184–205; Luzzatti, *Memorie*, pp. 249–55; Salvemini, *La politica estera di Francesco Crispi*, p. 56; Billot, *La France et l'Italie*, pp. 130–65.

of parliamentary crises in 1888 and 1889 through the sheer fact that there was nobody who could replace him. Hence, to some extent at least, Crispi's policy of pinpricks was envisaged as a means of alleviating his parliamentary position by persuading the French to make commercial concessions. This was the aspect which most struck foreign observers in Rome and certainly on his return from Friedrichsruhe:

> he indulged in arrogant and contemptuous language towards France, talking of bringing her to her knees in the commercial negotiations.

But this Crispi never achieved as the French, instead of accepting his terms, gradually pushed up their own. By January 1888 it had become clear in Paris that Italy had joined some sort of Mediterranean League directed against them and the arrival of high-ranking Italian Army officers in Berlin led to the further conclusion, correct as it transpired, that Italy was making a military alliance with Germany. In these circumstances the French saw no reason to make concessions to Crispi and as it became clear that the results of tariff war, whilst disastrous for Italy, were of much less importance for France, successive French foreign ministers demanded as their price for the concessions Crispi wanted, first the settlement of all Tunisian difficulties, then Italy's withdrawal from the Triple Alliance.[1]

But if the tariff war lay at the root of the series of incidents between France and Italy in 1888–9 no less important was Crispi's own outlook, character and temperament. Crispi the Foreign Minister and Crispi the follower of Mazzini were indistinguishable: he could never shake off the days of his youth which he had spent as a conspirator in exile, with a love for travelling incognito and dramatic personal interviews which were to change the face of Europe. He affected to despise most Italian diplomats as aristocratic incompetents and far preferred to send his own special emissaries travelling around Europe and

---

[1] Billot, ibid.; D.D.F., VII, Nos. 310, 316, 324, Annexe I; VIII, No. 183; Kennedy, Dering, Dufferin to Salisbury 31 January, 21 February 1888; 1 March 1889; 8 February 1890, F.O., 45/601, Nos. 16, 41;/623, No. 52;/ 646, No. 24. By February 1888 the situation was so bad that Crispi had to urge Berlin to take up Italian securities: Crispi to Launay 20 February 1888, A.M.E., Tel. 126.194.

to obtain his information from his own secret contacts, particularly from his old conspiratorial acquaintances in Paris. This attitude, a heritage of his Mazzinian past, was not without its effects upon the formulation and execution of Italian foreign policy in the later 1880's, with much consequent confusion. Moreover, authoritarian by nature, in complete command of his Cabinet in which he held the three key offices of President of the Council, the Interior and Foreign Affairs, Crispi gradually acquired an unshakeable position in Parliament. There was a general conviction that Italy had at last found a statesman who would sweep away the corruption and futility which had characterised politics under his immediate predecessors and, whilst acting within the constitution, would exercise a sort of dictatorship which would achieve a species of miracle. Even Robilant who refused to serve under him and regarded him as 'a minor Bismarck', had to admit that he was the only man who could govern Italy in 1887. But, effective though he was in internal affairs, Crispi's temperament was disastrous in a Foreign Minister. A good mob orator, Crispi was accustomed to addressing his audiences in somewhat intemperate language, both in or out of power, a habit which frequently provoked violent incidents in the Italian Chamber. It never seemed to occur to him when he became Foreign Minister to adopt different methods, with the result that he harangued foreign diplomats in Rome in the same manner as he treated both his Cabinet colleagues and the Italian Parliament, with obvious effect upon their reports. Uxkull, the Russian minister, after a distinctly trying session with Crispi, was particularly annoyed:

> Tout cela ce sont des phrases dont il se sert pour agrandir sa personne et surtout pour donner satisfaction à l'orgueil italien, qui ne sait où donner de la tête pour qu'on prenne au serieux sa position de grande puissance.[1]

Crispi's attitude to France was a series of contradictions. On the one hand he had a genuine regard for French civilisation and for the French people, to whom he frequently paid tribute

[1] Bruck to Kálnoky 18 October 1887, S.A.W., XI, 98.60B; Chabod, pp. 110, 555, 612, 636–45; Salvemini, p. 41; Croce, *History of Italy 1874–1914*– p. 165; Kennedy to Salisbury 26 August 1887; 31 January 1888, F.O., 45/576, No. 232;/601, No. 16.

in his public speeches, notably in October 1887 at Turin on his return from Friedrichsruhe when he declared:

> nobody could want a war between our two countries since either victory or defeat would be equally disastrous to the freedom of our two peoples and destructive of the equilibrium of Europe.

But here again Crispi the Mazzinian was the equal of Crispi the statesman. He felt no particular gratitude to France for Magenta or Solferino, only annoyance at the persistence of French moral tutelage over Italy: convinced that Italian independence depended upon a break with this French tradition, when the chance came in 1870 Crispi had been amongst the first to raise the cry of Nice and Savoy and to demand a military alliance with Prussia-Germany. Assuming that Italy had been made by the awakening of the Italian people to their destiny as the heirs of ancient Rome, Crispi was convinced that Italy was entitled to her position as a great power, resented French assumptions of superiority and was determined to assert Italian rights in the Mediterranean:

> France must forget the days of her influence beyond the Alps and must recognise that Italy is her equal in the concert of nations.

But as Salvemini, the most severe of Crispi's critics, points out, it is unlikely that he actually carried his mistrust of France to the extent of planning war in collaboration with Bismarck. Apart from anything else Crispi was not the cold, calculating planner, he was a man of impulse, temperamental and obsessed with his own preconceptions. Assuming that France was about to attack him, he prepared to defend himself by his military convention with Bismarck, little realising the economic consequences. Feeling hemmed in by French superiority in the Mediterranean, he lashed out on every issue in which Italian prestige was remotely involved.[1]

Crispi's 'alarums and excursions', despite their exaggerated form, were however based on some genuine danger of war. This lay, mainly, in the instability of republican government in

---

[1] Crispi, *Politica Estera*, p. 184, *Pensieri e Profezie*, p. 183; Salvemini, pp. 46, 54; Chabod, pp. 14, 52, 460–3; Jemolo, *Crispi*, pp. 47–50, 112.

France where, after the 1885 elections, at least three groups jostled for power. The belief that the constitutional question had been settled in 1887 by the quiet assumption of power by the respectable, moderate, republican groups around Ferry, Freycinet and Gambetta—the so-called Opportunists—was rudely shattered by the agricultural depression of the early eighties. At the 1885 elections this was ably exploited in the country-side by the Conservative, Monarchist, leaders so as to bring a serious revival of their power in the Chamber. Since the Radicals under Clemenceau, in this period a party of social reform with its main support in the large towns, similarly exploited the cry of 'Ferry, le Tonkinois', the Opportunists could no longer form a government on their own. From 1885–9 government had to be a coalition, and it was out of this *mêlée* that emerged the figure of General Boulanger who first came to power as a Radical general, Clemenceau's candidate for Minister of War, whom the Opportunists had to accept as the price of Radical support. For the next four years the ups and downs of Boulanger were of international concern, since he increasingly identified himself with the idea of a war of revenge against Germany and, magnified by Bismarck's sabre-rattling during the winter of 1886–7, rapidly became a popular hero. Increasingly after 1887 he managed to square the circle by attracting Monarchist as well as Radical support, and the fear that he would emerge as a new Bonaparte who would inaugurate a general European war, was by no means imaginary.[1]

If France were to attack, Italy would be covered by the Triple Alliance and in the long run Germany would no doubt be victorious, but the trouble was that in the meantime Italy, with her long coastline, would be completely exposed to the ravages of the French Mediterranean Fleet. Hence Crispi's interest in military and naval conventions and his frequent panics at reports from Paris of the imminence of some Boulangist *coup*, particularly as Boulanger and his new Monarchist friends became increasingly associated with Crispi's long-standing bugbear, the 'Black International'. Any Italian Government would have been alarmed at such reports; fear that the French Right would intervene in Italy in favour of a restoration of the Tempo-

[1] Dansette, *Le Boulangisme*, pp. 1–226. For Crispi's fears in this respect see *Politica Estera*, pp. 226–35, 300–5.

ral Power had haunted the Quirinal since 1870 and had been partly responsible for the decision to negotiate with Berlin in 1882; but Crispi, as usual, exaggerated. As a disciple of Mazzini, Crispi always regarded the Church as the major opponent of the new Italian State and habitually attributed both internal and external difficulties to its intrigues. This habit of searching for Jesuits under every bed led him to some very curious results, not the least of which was his transformation from an ardent irredentist into a firm supporter of the Habsburg Empire, as he wrote to Nigra, the Italian Ambassador in Vienna, in 1890:

> Italy must have her frontiers secure. Since she cannot, unfortunately, have French friendship at present she must at all costs hold on to Austria and not compromise the alliance. If Austria got away from us she would ally herself at once with France in defence of the Pope. The consequences of this would be incalculable.

In this frame of mind it is not surprising that the association of Boulanger with the lunatic fringe of the French Right convinced Crispi that war was imminent. As Billot, the French Ambassador in Rome and hardly an admirer, pointed out, Crispi was perfectly sincere: he was simply 'the victim of his own temperament'.[1]

Crispi's fears and surmises in themselves, however, do not explain the seriousness of the crises of 1888: behind them lay one solid fact, French naval predominance in the Mediterranean. During the Second Empire the French Navy had been in the forefront of the technical advances which had swept away the old wooden walls of Trafalgar and brought in the age of the steam-powered ironclad, measures which had inspired frequent naval panics in England and considerable expenditure in order to keep up. But with the French defeat in the war of 1870 and her concentration in the years that followed upon recovering military parity with Germany, all cause for alarm in England had died down, with a corresponding fall off in the Naval Estimates, so that when from 1878 onwards the French

[1] Billot, p. 128; Chabod, pp. 121, 361, 477; Val Cismon, *Lo scioglimento della Pro Patria di Trento nel carteggio Crispi-Nigra* in *Rassegna storica del Risorgimento*, 1934, fasc. I, p. 14; Dering to Salisbury 23 July 1889, F.O., 45/624, No. 159.

inaugurated a new policy of naval construction, which by 1885 had brought them a fleet of some twenty-five first-class iron-clads built or building, this fleet was in all respects comparable to that of England. Increasingly from 1887 onwards, as the evidence flowed into Paris of the close military co-operation between Italy and Germany, this fleet was concentrated at Toulon, with the result that by April 1888 the French had fourteen ironclads in the Mediterranean, which were steadily increased to twenty by 1891. It was this situation which so alarmed Crispi because the Italian Fleet was much smaller.

Admiral Brin, the Italian Minister of Marine throughout the 1880's and the chief inspirer of her naval construction, had deliberately gone in for large battleships—in the later eighties Italy possessed the largest in the world—and home construction. This policy had of course the advantage of building up an Italian naval industry which, by 1888, was supplying even the armour and engines for the latest battleships; but it had inevitably meant slowness of construction. Moreover, the monster guns on the new battleships gave considerable trouble and, more serious, there was a severe shortage of trained personnel. This was so marked, Admiral Lovera told Beresford, as to seriously impair the fighting value of the fleet:

> The ships are good but the personnel are *absolutely* useless. They knuckle down and pray to Heaven in a gale, and Heaven never has and never will steer the ships or secure the boats without assistance. Aves and Paters are excellent additions to energy and muscle, but no protection against shot and shell.[1]

In this situation the Italian Fleet was obviously no match for the French, who reckoned to be able to man their entire fleet at forty-eight hours' notice, and Brin, for one, thought the situation hopeless. French strategists of the *Jeune Ecole* in the eighties made no secret of the fact that their policy would be to achieve a quick decision by the bombardment of coastal towns, which, as Brin recognised, the Italians with their long and unfortified coastline were powerless to prevent. The Italian Fleet would be forced by public pressure to intervene, suffer inevitable defeat,

[1] Beresford to Balfour 21 December 1891, B.P., Add. MSS. 49713; Salisbury to Kennedy 22 March 1888, F.O., 170/400, No. 105; Marder, *The Anatomy of British Sea Power*, pp. 119–44.

leaving the French masters of the Mediterranean and free to transport troops from Algeria to any point they wished in Italy.[1]

In these circumstances Crispi's desperate anxiety to make a naval convention with his allies and, more important, since their fleets were negligible, to enlist their support in obtaining a naval alliance with England, becomes readily understandable and the occasion for his approaches to London in February and March 1888 lay in the belief that the build-up of the French Fleet at Toulon heralded an imminent strike. This rumour, which originated in the German Embassy in Paris, was passed on to Crispi on 3 February by Menabrea, the Italian Ambassador, along with his belief that a Boulangist *coup d'état* was imminent. Crispi immediately relayed this to London as a request for British naval support, a request which was backed by the German Embassy. Salisbury received this on 4 February and, according to Catalani, the Italian Chargé d'Affaires, was considerably impressed:

> in accordance with his promise Salisbury, immediately after our interview yesterday addressed a note to the Admiralty to give orders for the reinforcement of the British squadron in the Mediterranean. The Prime Minister's note contained all the details in your Excellency's telegram of 1st February. His Lordship has met the First Lord of the Admiralty and has recommended that all measures of precaution should be taken in the interests both of England and of Italy. Telegrams have been sent to Paris and Toulon to obtain fuller information. In a report of 2nd February Lord Lytton (the British Ambassador in Paris) was of the opinion that the French armaments were aimed only at putting the French Fleet, which had recently been reduced, upon a normal footing.[2]

The Admiralty, whilst prepared to investigate further the activity at Toulon, were not inclined to take these reports at their face value. Hamilton, the First Lord, thought the alarm vastly exaggerated but offered, if Salisbury thought it necessary to reassure the Italians, to send the Channel Squadron, which was already in the Mediterranean, on a visit to Genoa and

[1] Kennedy to Salisbury 22 September, 12 December 1888, F.O., 45/603, Nos. 248, 338.

[2] Catalani to Crispi 5 February 1888, A.M.E., Seria Politica, 29/1985; Crispi, *Politica Estera*, pp. 226–35; G.P., VI, p. 207.

Spezia for a week or so, a decision which produced Admiral Hewitt's celebrated demonstration at Genoa on 15 February. When towards the end of March Crispi's fears that something was in the air again revived—French naval officers disguised as artists were reputed to be haunting Spezia—German pressure was brought to bear upon Salisbury again to reinforce the Mediterranean Fleet and once more the Channel Squadron was ordered to Genoa, apparently this time on the Admiralty's own initiative.[1]

The importance of these diplomatic manoeuvres and fleet movements of February and March 1888 lies in the extent to which they achieved Crispi's aim of transforming the agreements of 1887 into a naval alliance. Crispi fully believed that he had succeeded in this. Throughout this period, according to Bruck, the Austrian Ambassador in Rome, he appeared to put complete trust in his secret agreement with England and took it for granted that 'in event of war England must give Italy naval support whatever happened'. He spoke quite openly of the sending of the English Channel Fleet into the Mediterranean as a warning to France, a warning which alone had deterred her from an attack upon Genoa, which, he asserted, she was planning to seize as her first object in a war against Italy. But Crispi's claims went further than this. On 14 April he announced that:

> through the intervention of Prince Bismarck an exact agreement has been reached by which in case of a French attack on Italy the English Fleet would immediately take action on behalf of the latter power.[2]

It is important to determine how much truth there was in this since, if Crispi's statement can be relied upon, Salisbury had made an absolutely binding commitment.

One thing is clear, there was no pressure for an Italian alliance from the Admiralty who were convinced that nothing out of the ordinary was going on: if it were left to him, Hamilton would have preferred to take no action since in his view it would only alarm the French unnecessarily. Whilst it is possible that

[1] Hamilton to Salisbury 5 February, Salisbury to Edinburgh 27 March Scott to Salisbury 31 March 1888, S.P.; G.P., VI, Nos. 1789–91.

[2] Bruck to Kálnoky 26 February, 14, 21 April 1888, S.A.W., Geheimakten XXIV/1, Fasz. Rot, 463/20C, Tel. 81, 40C.

Salisbury took this first alarm more seriously—this was, after all, his first experience of Crispi crying 'wolf'—even this is doubtful: as early as 8 February he told the Austrian Ambassador in London, Károlyi, that he could see no reason for Italian fears. Why then did he order a naval demonstration? His reasoning emerges from a letter he wrote to the Duke of Edinburgh, Commander of the Mediterranean Fleet, at the end of March:

> Six weeks ago there was a scare by Crispi about the supposed preparations at Toulon and I asked the Admiralty to send the Fleet to Genoa and Spezia for a week or two, but there is nothing at present to justify such a step.
>
> Germany is playing a double game; they may be deceiving us as well as Russia but I lean strongly to the other belief—that Austria is a necessity to her and that all other motives in European politics are made to bend to that necessity . . . to sustain Austria she will be willing to push on Austrian policy in Bulgaria and on the Bosphorus, though the matter is indifferent to Germany: and that is, no doubt, the secret of the efforts she has made to provide Austria with allies in the shape of Italy and England.
>
> If Russia looks like occupying Bulgaria your job is to consider forcing the Dardanelles.
>
> Egypt is quiet. Franco-Italian antipathy is strengthening. The Germans are always impressing upon me that the sole chance of Italy being able to help Austria in the event of an attack by Russia on Austria would be that her coasts should be protected by us from French naval attack. Without our naval alliance the Germans always maintain that Italy would count for nothing and be paralysed.[1]

In other words this was a gesture aimed less at warning the French than at reassuring the Italians: it seems that neither Salisbury nor the Admiralty thought the situation as serious as Crispi claimed or sufficiently alarming to warrant a naval alliance.

This view is confirmed by French sources. The French, vitally interested and made nervous by the rumours they had already received of Italian military negotiations at Berlin and of British adhesion to the Triple Alliance, got wind of Crispi's approaches to London almost as soon as they were made and

[1] Salisbury to Edinburgh 27 March, Hamilton to Salisbury 5 February, S.P.

Waddington, the French Ambassador in London, was sent to sound out leading Liberals who were presumed to be pro-French, and to take up the question formally with Salisbury. France, he explained, was interested only in the maintenance of the *status quo*, she was not indulging in any extraordinary armaments but only taking some defensive precautions against the unusual activity in Italy. What truth Waddington then asked was there in the current rumours? Salisbury was quite reassuring; the Channel Squadron's visit to Genoa was all part of its Mediterranean cruise into which nothing unusual should be read: whilst recognising Crispi's agitated temperament he thought French fears unjustified, adding, 'on this side, as on the other, you are too nervous'.[1] But unfortunately for Salisbury, Waddington had attacked on two fronts: on the same evening as his first interview at the Foreign Office, Labouchère, the editor of *Truth*, a Liberal back-bencher notorious for his pro-French sympathies, launched an inspired denunciation of any engagements with the Central Powers, demanding to know what commitments Salisbury had made. Whilst to Waddington Salisbury could formally deny the existence of any engagements with Bismarck, in the House of Commons, in what would be a public declaration, he had to be more circumspect, since an outright denial would be an effective repudiation of the 1887 agreements, a repudiation he dare not risk in view of the position at Constantinople. But in view of the fact that his Government depended upon the support of a large number of former Liberal M.P.s who had much the same views as Labouchère on foreign policy, he could not formally admit their existence either. Consequently Fergusson, the Parliamentary Under-Secretary, was instructed to hedge: on 14 February he denied that there was any engagement promising material action (a statement whose effect was rather ruined by Admiral Hewitt's demonstration at Genoa on the following day), then, on 22 February, when pressed again, finally stated that:

> we were under no engagements pledging the employment of the Military and Naval Forces in this country, except such as are already known to the House.[2]

[1] D.D.F., VII, Nos. 5, 41, 42, Annexe I.
[2] Hansard, 3rd series, Vol. CCCXXII, pp. 1172–94: *Letters of Queen Victoria*, I, p. 386.

If this appeared to satisfy the Leaders of the Opposition, to a trained observer like Waddington it gave the game away: it was clear, from the language used by Fergusson that at least an exchange of views had taken place, directed either against France or Russia and concerning the Mediterranean, probably boiling down to a defence of what Salisbury called 'England's traditional interests' in that area. But, he said, Granville had been quite explicit that Salisbury could not possibly have entered into any firm engagement promising material action in the event of war, because the House and the electorate would certainly repudiate them in the case of war against France unless France were to offer the direct insult.[1]

The accuracy of Waddington's appreciation of the situation was reflected in Italian dissatisfaction. Damiani, Crispi's *chef de cabinet*, informed Kennedy, the British Chargé d'Affaires at Rome, on 5 March that whilst he well understood Fergusson's statesmanlike reticence:

> both he and Crispi would have preferred some distinct allusion
> to British sympathies and promises of support towards Italy.[2]

Since he went on to speak of how secure Italy would feel if only she was certain of the support of the British Fleet, it is a fair deduction that, for all Crispi's airing of his secret agreement with Salisbury, he was still far from certain at the beginning of March of getting automatic naval support. If then there was any truth at all in Crispi's declarations they must refer to some statement made by Salisbury during the second of the two scares, at the end of March. This conclusion is reinforced by the Austrian correspondence.

Kálnoky, directly interested in anything which helped to bind the somewhat suspect Crispi to the alliance with the Central Powers, set to work to verify the story as reported by Bruck. Highly sceptical both of Crispi's assumptions as to the impending French attacks and of Salisbury's reported reaction to this, he got Károlyi to raise the subject in London. Since Salisbury discounted completely any chance of such a French attack and made no mention whatsoever of any agreement with Italy— leading Károlyi to suspect that the whole thing was a piece of

[1] D.D.F., VII, Nos. 42, 60, 69.
[2] Kennedy to Salisbury 5 March 1888, F.O., 45/601, No. 55.

Crispi's imagination—Kálnoky now checked with Berlin and the whole story emerged:

> a short while ago the Italian Government was in great fear of an immediate French attack by land and sea on Spezia (a fear which to me seems quite baseless). As a result of this alarm the German Government, in whose interest it lies that Italy should be secure against French attacks, raised the question with Lord Salisbury of the possible protection of the Italian coasts against France through English seapower, with particular reference to a completely unprovoked attack. Whereupon Lord Salisbury, (who equally shares my doubts of the likelihood of such a project on the part of France) gave the assurance that in such a case the English Fleet would immediately come to the help of the Italian Fleet. In the despatch that was read to me there was no question of a formal agreement having been reached and so Baron Bruck in his telegraphic report that 'a precise agreement has been reached' over the form of Lord Salisbury's assurance is not completely correct.[1]

From this it is clear that, as usual, Crispi was exaggerating: clearly Salisbury had made no precise agreement, he had merely stated verbally that in certain circumstances he would protect Italy with the British Fleet. True that this was in some degree an advance upon the vague terms of the Note of February 1887 and that to this extent Crispi had made some progress in his attempt to make an English alliance: and it may well be, as Bruck forecast, that in his usual optimism he convinced himself that the alliance was as good as made and that he could now provoke France with impunity. But if so he made a bad mistake. In the first place British naval support in the Mediterranean was by no means so automatic as he assumed as Salisbury, reflecting War Office views, told Hatzfeldt on 24 April that in case of war with France the British Fleet would be needed in the Channel.[2] Secondly, he completely misread Salisbury's intentions, since it was precisely Crispi's misplaced bellicosity during the next six months which ruined what chance there was of the Anglo-Italian understanding developing into an alliance at the end of the year.

[1] Kálnoky to Károlyi 15, 29 April, Károlyi to Kálnoky 25 April 1888, S.A.W., Geheimakten XXIV/1, Fasz. Rot, 463/14A–D.
[2] G.P., VI, p. 209 note.

Consideration of such an alliance in London in December 1888 was the direct outcome of the naval situation as it revealed itself in the course of the summer. In the 1880's naval construction in England had been bedevilled by rival theories as to the future of naval warfare. On the one hand the adherents of the battleship who advocated the building of bigger and bigger battleships with more and more armour and better and better guns; on the other hand the adherents of the torpedo who considered that this new weapon had put an end to the monster battleship and who advocated the construction of more and more torpedo boats, cruisers for commerce protection, and so on; a view shared even by the Armstrong Ordnance Works of Elswick whose vested interest in armour plate was considerable. The result was paralysis in the Board of Admiralty who were completely uncertain as to the way in which things would develop. As the First Lord put it in 1884:

> the great difficulty the Admiralty would have to contend with, if they were granted three or four millions tomorrow for the purpose referred to would be to decide how they would spend the money.[1]

Consequently there was considerable resistance from the Board of Admiralty to any large-scale expenditure on ironclads which, they were only too well aware, might well become completely outdated within ten years. One of the curiosities of the situation in 1888 is that the Board of Admiralty themselves were not in any way involved in the pressure for naval expansion: in fact as late as March of that year Hamilton, the First Lord, gave the probability of obsolescence as quite sufficient reason for their reluctance to build on a large scale.[2]

Allied to this were Admiralty views on strategy. They took it as axiomatic that the enemy in the next war, as always in the past, would be France and although endowed with a healthy respect for the value of the French Fleet they were highly sceptical whether it would ever risk battle: it seemed obvious to the Board that the French could achieve much the best results by fighting a *guerre de course*, as in fact the *Jeune Ecole* advocated, which of course gave further support to those who thought of

[1] Hansard, 3rd series, CCXC, 661–2 (10 July 1884).
[2] Marder, pp. 123–6.

naval construction in terms of cruisers and torpedo boats. This came out very clearly in the war scare in February 1888 when the First Lord, replying to Salisbury's request for reinforcements for the Mediterranean Fleet, wrote:

> this alarm is exaggerated: they have nothing like the necessary number of ships to cause trouble. Anyway if the French mean business it is not to the Mediterranean but to China and Australasia that reinforcements should go, as our commerce can be hit.[1]

This in fact was one reason why throughout 1888 the Admiralty were so highly reluctant to reinforce the Mediterranean Fleet since, as they pointed out to Edinburgh when he requested reinforcement in January, to be at all effective he needed at least another ten ironclads and to supply these would be to seriously weaken the remaining British forces in the Channel. Instead their idea was to leave a weak Mediterranean Squadron and a powerful Channel Squadron based on Gibraltar which could cruise around and mop up any French Fleet escaping from the Mediterranean: this they thought the only possible strategy to pursue since the blockade of Toulon would take far more ships than Britain in fact possessed, as the blockading force always needed at least a 3 to 2 superiority.[2]

The combined result then of Admiralty building policy and strategy was that England could not expect to control the Mediterranean in the event of war, a fact which as Salisbury was later to remark, made nonsense of current foreign policy. This was bad enough, but there was worse to follow. Uncertainty as to future development had led the Board to adopt a compromise form of construction, the so-called 'soft ender', an ironclad with armour plate only in the centre of the ship, which led to increasing criticism and predictions that the French would sink the lot. This fact, coupled with Admiralty ideas of sending the Channel Fleet off to Gibraltar, now aroused the War Office sufficiently for them to launch an invasion scare and join the naval critics in a public demand for a vast increase in expenditure upon defence. Just how far the Admiralty's critics were justified it is difficult to assess since in 1888 they were never put

[1] Hamilton to Salisbury 5 February 1888, S.P.
[2] Marder, pp. 129–30.

to the acid test of a war with France, but competent observers thought that the fighting quality of the British Fleet was at its lowest ebb since the mid-eighteenth century and that the technical deficiencies were such that the French would have made mincemeat of anything opposed to them.[1] Beresford, who resigned as Fourth Sea Lord at the end of 1887 to lead the campaign for naval expansion, was one of the fiercest critics of the current Admiralty construction policy of the so-called 'soft enders', criticism in which he was supported by Admirals Hoskins and Richards who both became First Sea Lord in the nineties. These ships with their armoured vitals but unarmoured ends, were regarded by Beresford as a death-trap. He wrote home from the Mediterranean in 1891 :

> All the French battleships are belted all round, seven out of our eleven are floated by Sardine box ends. If we have a big action out here, think kindly of us floating the wrong way up "With Care" like a railway parcel.[2]

In 1888 he took his criticisms so far as to propose in the House of Commons that one of these unarmoured ended battleships should be thoroughly and practically tried by perforating its ends and placing it in the same position as it would probably occupy in an action, a motion which he was asked to withdraw by a member of the Cabinet on the grounds that if it turned out that his theory was correct:

> do you think it would be to the advantage of England to show other nations that thirteen out of twenty-two of her first class battleships are inferior to those of France and that they can be made dangerous from small gun fire ?[3]

Despite the increasing public alarm and campaign in the Conservative Press Beresford found it still uphill work to convince the House of Commons and the Cabinet that something should be done. A select committee of the House was eventually appointed to undertake a survey of the strength of the fleet but the Admiralty evidence was all to the effect that there was nothing to worry about: the First Lord still insisted in June that

[1] Ibid., pp. 71–76, 132–8.
[2] Beresford to Balfour 21 December 1891, B.P., Add. MSS. 49713.
[3] Ibid., 10 September 1891.

the French were making no preparations of any exceptional kind but were simply refitting their existing ironclad fleet which had been neglected in the past, a fact from which he took great comfort since it meant that so much less money was available for new building, leaving, he thought, a balance in our favour.[1] Even Salisbury, pressed by the Queen about the very 'unsatisfactory state' of the Navy, took the view that the only real deficiency was in the slowness of production of guns for the new ships building and seemed completely unperturbed by the French menace which was currently alarming the public. As he pointed out, in his view France was no danger to England as long as her relations with Germany and Italy were so bad, it was only when these relations improved that 'the Army and Navy Estimates would rise very rapidly'.[2] Yet by the end of the year his Cabinet had approved the largest measures of naval defence yet seen in peacetime—twenty million pounds over the next four years on new ships alone—and by the adoption of the Two Power standard forged a new phase of British naval policy which lasted until 1921.

Two factors largely explained this sudden change of heart. In the first place the Naval Intelligence Division of the Admiralty and an independent enquiry launched simultaneously by three leading Admirals became increasingly uneasy at the prospect of Russian collaboration with France in the Mediterranean. It was already apparent that they were working hand-in-glove at Constantinople, whilst the rising demand for a Russian alliance conducted by the Boulangists, coupled with the first Russian loans on the Paris Bourse, made this seem not unlikely. According to the three Admirals the lesson of the summer manoeuvres of 1888 was that the fleet was altogether inadequate to blockade even the French, whilst if England had to reckon on taking on France and Russia combined, the balance of maritime strength would be against her. Consequently they joined the N.I.D. in advocating a construction programme which would put England beyond comparison with any two powers, coming down heavily in favour of the ironclad battleship as the dominating influence at sea. It was these proposals which produced the ratios 6 to 5 in the first class ships, $4\frac{1}{2}$ to 2 in second class ships as against France

[1] Hamilton to Salisbury 18 June 1888, S.P.
[2] Salisbury to the Queen 12 June, 25 August 1888, *Letters*, I, pp. 436–8.

and Russia combined, which were adopted in the Naval Defence Act of March 1889.[1]

This evidence of an expert opinion divergent from that held by the Board, added to the public clamour led by people like Beresford, certainly made some members of the Cabinet uneasy.[2] But the final push that determined Cabinet action came, as usual, from Bismarck. Throughout the year he had been urging that the Mediterranean Fleet be strengthened, but during the autumn German representations in London took on a new note. England, Bismarck urged, must live up to her responsibilities as a Great Power: if she expected assistance from the Triple Alliance to defend her Mediterranean interests, then she must be in a position to reciprocate. In other words she must both strengthen her fleet and, preferably, defend her interests by joining the 'League of Peace' since such a combination would provide sufficient deterrent to check any potential action of France and Russia combined.[3]

The explanation of Bismarck's intervention at this juncture reflects Germany's external and internal problems in 1888. All the indications are that the Chancellor was strongly opposed to war. As he explained to Crispi in October, before Germany went to war it must be an issue which fully aroused the support of the peace-loving German people, not mere diplomatic incidents such as the Tunis schools affair.[4] But, if Bismarck was opposed to war, he could equally ill afford to lose the Italian alliance or, what he seemed to regard as synonymous, Crispi directing Italian affairs. Hence the effort had to be made to satisfy Crispi and Italian demands as much as possible, particularly if these could be exploited to bring in England, the 'cement' of the Triple Alliance. These considerations were reinforced by Bismarck's main internal problem, his relations with the military politicians. Both Moltke and his successor, Waldersee, were insistent that they must assume a two front war: further, that in view of the extent of French fortifications they must base their war planning on an immediate attack upon Russia, a conclusion which led them to press increasingly for a 'preventive war'.

[1] Marder, pp. 111, 131–2, 161.
[2] Beresford to Balfour 4 May 1896, B.P., Add. MSS. 49713.
[3] G.P., IV, No. 942; VI, No. 1281.
[4] G.P., VI, No. 1287.

Whilst Bismarck may not have feared the eventual outcome—he told Crispi in August 1888 that whilst he preferred peace he was not afraid of war—he strongly opposed any action which made war inevitable: he characterised Waldersee's ideas as committing suicide for fear of eventual death. Hence his object was not to incite France and Russia to attack in order to destroy them, as Waldersee glibly proposed: as he pointed out, France had been destroyed in 1870 yet within five years she was a major power again. Waldersee's ideas of destroying Russia were chimerical: how, Bismarck asked, could you do this? The result would only be to create such a hatred of Germany in Russia that, added to the existing alienation of France, the European position of Germany would become impossible. On the contrary, Bismarck's ambition was to make the German position so strong diplomatically that France would be deterred from attacking and the obvious way to do this was by adding England to the Triple Alliance.[1] Since his attempts to achieve this indirectly by a firm Anglo-Italian naval understanding had been inconclusive, and encouraged by Hatzfeldt's reports of Salisbury's friendly attitude towards Germany, he now came out with the idea he had first aired to Disraeli ten years before—a direct Anglo-German alliance.[2]

In the circumstances of the end of 1888, with the Russian armies concentrating in Poland and Boulanger on the fringe of power in Paris, this was not an unreasonable proposition. Even some members of Salisbury's Cabinet regarded it as 'the best tonic for both countries and for European peace'.[3] As far as Anglo-German relations were concerned the time was as propitious as any. Apart from minor irritations over Zanzibar nothing had arisen to disturb the fundamental community of interest which Salisbury had noted at the beginning of the year:

> it is necessary to insist that our policy is identical with that of the Central Powers. England and Germany and to a great extent Austria are satisfied Powers. France and Russia are

[1] Rassow, *Die Stellung Deutschlands im Kreise der Grossen Mächte*, 1887–90, pp. 198–214; Ritter, *The Schlieffen Plan*, pp. 20–22; H.P., III, Nos. 244, 250. Crispi, *Politica Estera*, p. 264.

[2] Israel, *England und der Orientalische Dreibund* p. 25.

[3] G.P., IV, Nos. 944–5; for current alarm over Boulanger see Crispi, *Politica Estera*, pp. 300–5.

'hungry' Powers. Italy it is true is eminently a hungry Power: but the objects of her appetite are no great matter to us.[1]

As far as Crispi's agitations were concerned, Salisbury believed Bismarck innocent, as he had written to Malet in September:

> The great trouble of the hour seems to be Signor Crispi. I think I am not wrong in assuming that Germany does not want war just now and that therefore they take the same view of Crispi's proceedings as we do. Ct. Hatzfeldt is constantly impressing upon me that, odious and tiresome as Crispi is, he is the only minister who can be trusted to do the behests of the German powers and therefore must be supported.[2]

The marked reserve of German policy during the Tunis affair was equally welcome in London and made sufficient of an impression upon Salisbury that he could assure the French at the time that they were in no danger. Bismarck's sudden interest in Bizerta made him a little suspicious in January 1889, but there was nothing here to cause a rift.[3] Fundamentally therefore Hatzfeldt was correct in his appraisal of the situation: Salisbury *was* reasonably favourable towards German policy at this time. But this didn't mean that he wanted a German alliance. In the first place, if favourable towards German policy, Salisbury still retained some dislike of German personnel. In April this had brought a sharp outburst in protest against Bismarck over the Battenberg marriage project:

> The Chancellor's humours are as changeable as those of the French Assembly and you can never be certain that he will not try to levy a sort of diplomatic blackmail . . . unless you will do something to gratify some of his unreasonable personal antipathies.[4]

In October, similarly, on the occasion of the Imperial visit to Rome, he voiced his mistrust of the young Emperor to the French Chargé d'Affaires:

> Everything depends upon the effect that the Emperor and

[1] Salisbury to Morier 1 February 1888, S.P.

[2] Salisbury to Malet 1 September 1888, S.P.

[3] Minute by Salisbury on Lytton to Salisbury 3 January 1889, F.O., 27/2952, No. 2; D.D.F., VII, No. 247.

[4] Salisbury to Malet 11 April 1888, S.P.

Signor Crispi have upon each other, which is an extremely fragile guarantee of peace.[1]

But whilst these feelings may have had some effect upon Salisbury's attitude towards a German alliance, there can be little doubt that the real objection at this time lay in the impression of Italian aims current in London. Crispi, it was firmly believed, in contrast to Bismarck, was bent on war.

The Italy of Crispi was not the Italy of Robilant. When Salisbury had made his initial agreement in 1887 Italian foreign policy was in safe, conservative hands, but increasingly in 1888, under Crispi, it became less reliable and even began to clash with British interests. From this point of view the death of Robilant in October was a major disaster, as was recognised at the time, since even from the London Embassy he had been able to use his position of pre-eminence as an elder statesman to check Crispi's wilder extravagances: certainly he induced greater confidence in Italian policy than either his predecessor, Catalani, or his eventual successor, Tornielli, were able to command.[2] This lack of confidence was the main stumbling-block to an alliance since Salisbury increasingly feared that he would be dragged into one of Crispi's trumpery quarrels, a fear which was the direct outcome of the Massowa and Tunis schools incidents.

In both of these affairs the view was taken in London that Crispi was expanding minor differences, which were perfectly capable of solution if handled in a diplomatic manner, into major crises; a view which Robilant shared. Crispi's initial proposition that the régime of foreign capitulations should cease at Massowa now that it was governed by a civilised power was reasonable enough: difficulties arose when the French proposed to trade their acceptance for Italian recognition of the similar position in Tunis, where Crispi was always ultra-sensitive. Consequently, although at first, in July, Salisbury was inclined to support Crispi's viewpoint and advise the French to accept it,

[1] D.D.F., VII, No. 247. See also Cecil, IV, pp. 112–15.

[2] Kennedy to Salisbury 16 October, S.P.; Robilant was very popular in London: 'His tone rather led to the conclusion that in his view too much importance was attached to trivial questions in diplomatic communications generally, and especially in those which came from Italy.' Pauncefote to Kennedy 10 August 1888, F.O., 170/401, No. 169; Chabod, p. 636.

when, in August, Crispi blew this up out of all proportion and began to employ the bludgeon of Berlin to force the French to recognise his *fait accompli*, his attitude changed rapidly:

> I am very much afraid that unless he learns to employ more usual language and to bluster less he will lead the alliance into trouble. We have made a communication to the French Government to some extent in the sense which Ct. Bismarck desires. But I would not assume to advise the French Government to submit to that of Italy in this matter, because I should have thereby undertaken a certain amount of responsibility for the fresh insults which, on the first possible occasion, I have no doubt Signor Crispi will heap upon the French.[1]

This in turn affected Salisbury's standpoint over Tunis where, as Crispi rightly feared, Goblet staged his riposte for the Massowa affair. Throughout August Crispi made approaches to London to concert policy in the event of some French action in this region but with no success, since, in the first place, Salisbury did not really care if the French were to increase their control over their protectorate, and, in any case, he could not see that this made much effective difference to Italy.[2] Hence his complete indifference to the Beylical decrees at the end of September which restricted the rights of foreign schools, a move which seemed to presage formal annexation, and which Crispi loudly proclaimed would mean war, and increasing sympathy with France in the war of nerves which followed. On 10 October he made this quite clear in an interview with the French Chargé, Jusserand, when he castigated Crispi as an *agent provocateur*, dominated by his murky past. The one ray of hope, he thought, was that:

> Crispi is not Italy. The King was extremely sincere in his desire to maintain peace: an attitude shared by people like General Robilant.[3]

It is not surprising that this affected Salisbury's general attitude towards the Italian alliance. Even Crispi had detected

[1] Salisbury to Scott 7 August 1888, S.P.

[2] A view which Robilant shared: Salisbury to Kennedy 17 August 1888, F.O., 170/401, No. 172.

[3] Crispi, *Politica Estera*, pp. 281–3; D.D.F., VII, No. 247.

a difference in the atmosphere in London, which, characteristically, he put down to some misapprehension on Salisbury's part and which he affected not to understand. Robilant, instructed from Rome to seek out the cause of their coolness, repeated tartly that it was quite simple:

> Salisbury told me that he had no wish to be dragged into a quarrel with France over such an absurd issue as the Capitulations at Massowa.[1]

That Crispi was prejudicing the Italian position in Europe by his needless antagonism of France was widely recognised by the end of 1888. At home, as the military commitments to Germany came to be translated into hard fact in the shape of budget deficits, as French commercial hostility became effective, criticism became general:

> They demand that Italy revert to the comparatively modest and conciliatory position which she held under Count Robilant and Signor Depretis.[2]

This view was also echoed in Vienna as Kálnoky grew alarmed at the signs of disharmony between London and Rome. In his view British support for Italy was the cement which held the Triple Alliance together: if Crispi alienated England by his unnecessary provocation of France, with whom Kálnoky, like Salisbury, was inclined to sympathise on this issue, then the Triple Alliance would collapse. In December Austrian reports from London insisted that in the current state of opinion it was unlikely that Italy would receive British naval support in the event of war. Everything depended upon the *casus belli*: if Italy were to be construed the aggressor, as at present she would, then there was no hope of public opinion permitting British assistance to her. If this were true, then it seemed obvious to Kálnoky that Crispi was leading the alliance to disaster and he lost no time in making this abundantly clear to Rome, warning Crispi to expect no Austrian assistance either if he went to war over Tunis.[3]

[1] Robilant to Crispi 15, 17 September 1888, A.M.E., Seria Politica, 29/1448.

[2] Kennedy to Salisbury 24 December 1888, F.O., 45/603, No. 338.

[3] Deym to Kálnoky, Kálnoky to Bruck 4, 22 December 1888, S.A.W., VIII, 105.46D; XI, 101, Geheime Weisung.

In these circumstances then the renewed Italian bid for a naval alliance, made precisely at this time, was bound to fail despite its advocacy in the navalist Press. It was not, as Marder suggests, simply traditional opposition in London to Continental entanglements: it would have been the height of madness for a Cabinet to have made an alliance whose main purpose was to ward off the dangers of war against France, with a partner currently engaged in provoking France over an issue in which England had not the slightest interest, and on which the Government could not possibly hope for public support. Salisbury was quite convinced at this time that Crispi's purpose was war since, he thought, the armed peace was financially ruinous to Italy and various hints had been dropped by Herbert Bismarck, amongst others, of their hopes of Nice, Savoy and Tunis. The effect of this conviction upon British policy in the Mediterranean was to introduce much greater caution, as Salisbury himself explained to Dufferin, newly appointed to the Rome Embassy at the end of the year:

> At first we were very cordial with Italy—which is our normal policy. But as Crispi's character developed we came to the conclusion that it was better to give him a wide berth. We have therefore kept out of his quarrels with France and declined to give any guarantees beyond a strong desire for the status quo in the Mediterranean. My impression is that if France attacked Italy gratuitously by sea, the English feeling would be in favour of going to her assistance, but that if a war were to arise out of one of Crispi's trumpery quarrels, England would certainly stand aloof.[1]

Although the decision to give 'Crispi a wide berth' didn't necessarily preclude a German alliance, this, added to Salisbury's doubts as to the personal qualities of the German leadership, made it much less attractive. True that it would 'solve' the Straits and Egyptian 'problems': but for the moment at least these were quiet, whilst on the debit side would be the lasting hostility of France, which it was no part of Salisbury's policy to incur.

[1] Salisbury to Dufferin 28 December 1888, S.P. The Italian approach was made via Brin, reported in Kennedy to Salisbury 12 December 1888, F.O., 45/603, No. 338, cited in Marder, p. 141, 'If only Italy had an alliance with England, I and many others with me, would feel perfectly secure.'

But even if Bismarck's proposition had been more attractive from the viewpoint of the Foreign Office, the deciding factor when it came to the point was the internal position of Salisbury's Government. The Conservative administration had struggled on since 1886 with a minority of Conservative M.P.s in the House of Commons, dependent upon an informal agreement with Hartington that he should support them with his so-called Unionists. But the Unionists themselves were far from being a homogeneous body: none of them, except Goschen, would enter the Cabinet, leaving them free of responsibility and in a better position to rejoin the fold of the Liberal Party if they could agree terms with Gladstone. To make matters worse, the Unionists really consisted of two parties, Hartington's and Chamberlain's, at daggers drawn over social reform which Chamberlain had been pressing since the 'unauthorised programme' of 1885.[1] This all came to a head at the end of 1888 because Smith, the Leader of the House, wanted to retire through ill health and the problem became how to replace him. The obvious candidate, Goschen, was ruled out because he would not join the Carlton and, as Balfour put it, because 'he cannot stay on the bench through mere fidgetiness, for ten minutes consecutively'. Since it was impossible to promote Balfour over Goschen's head— Goschen had been a Cabinet Minister before Balfour entered the House—this left only Hartington, who was thus in an extremely strong position: so much so that Balfour advocated coalition as the only way out of the Government's present position:

> And above all it would save us from the difficulties on which we have more than once nearly made shipwreck, the difficulties I mean arising from having a separate and irresponsible council of War directing the movements of one wing of the allied Army. This difficulty is not likely to diminish. It will become formidable again as soon as ambitious legislation is attempted. . . .[2]

With this the domestic position at the end of 1888, Salisbury was in no position to embark upon a major venture in foreign policy without the consent of his allies: Hartington thought the

[1] Balfour to Salisbury 24 July, Salisbury to Balfour 26 July 1892, B.P., Add. MSS. 49690.
[2] Balfour to Salisbury 23 December 1888, B.P., Add. MSS. 49689.

moment 'inopportune' for a German alliance, which effectively killed it. Instead the Cabinet took up the more popular naval programme, designed to reach the 'Two Power' standard by 1894, a decision which was reached by January and publicly announced in the Naval Defence Act of March 1889.[1] In this way although Bismarck's major request that Britain should enter the 'League of Peace' was rejected, his pressure had at least been effective in achieving his minor object, the strengthening of the British Fleet. The effect of this was to improve considerably the British negotiating position in Europe and to enhance her value as an alliance partner, with the result that even if the prospects of an alliance with Italy faded, 1889–92 were to be the years in which relations with Germany and the Triple Alliance in general reached their peak.

[1] Salisbury to Balfour 10 January 1889, ibid.; G.P., IV, Nos. 944–5.

III

SALISBURY
AND THE NEW COURSE

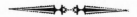

> . . . any indefinite postponement of a settlement in
> Africa would render it very difficult to maintain terms of
> amity with Germany, and would force us to change our
> system of alliances in Europe.
>
> Salisbury to the Queen, 1890.

SINCE Salisbury's return to office in 1886 British foreign
policy had been largely determined by Mediterranean
problems. In 1886–7 the major preoccupation had been the
danger of a Russian descent upon Constantinople, in 1888–9 the
main fear the outbreak of a Franco-Italian war. As a result of
these preoccupations Salisbury had first reached an understanding with Italy and Austria, then had initiated the Two
Power standard, measures which indicated clearly enough that
British policy was directed mainly against France and Russia,
the 'hungry' powers as he called them. Similarly in the case of
Germany. Despite the Re-Insurance treaty it is evident that
since 1887 Bismarck had been worried by the prospect of
Franco-Russian collaboration. At first he had tried to get round
this by the combination of on the one hand the German-inspired
Anglo-Italian alliance and on the other the secret agreement
with Russia, but his confidence in this arrangement would seem
to have been short lived. By October 1888 he was dropping
heavy hints that England should openly join the Triple Alliance:

He said that, if there had been that real defensive alliance
between England and the two Empires . . . Germany would

willingly have accepted any risk of displeasing Russia. . . .
But no such alliance exists.[1]

Finally he had come out openly with his suggestion of an Anglo-German alliance, which Salisbury had turned down. Up to 1889 therefore the Franco-Russian threat in the Mediterranean had forced England and Germany to collaborate, but it had not produced an alliance. To obtain British support for Italy, Bismarck had committed Germany to an alignment with England at Constantinople and at Cairo, support which was as useful to Salisbury as the British *quid pro quo*, the Mediterranean Fleet, was to Bismarck. The great question by 1890 was whether this mutually advantageous arrangement could continue, whether it could be developed into the alliance that Berlin wanted, or whether it would be ruined by the growing clash of interests in Africa.

The African problem in 1890 had two main aspects as far as Salisbury's relations with Europe were concerned, and it is worth pointing out, in view of the controversy over his purpose, that both derived from Mediterranean problems. In the first place there was the growing rivalry between British and German companies for the control of trade in East Africa. This had been settled once in 1886 by a division of the coastal strip, nominally belonging to the Sultan of Zanzibar, into British and German spheres, but by 1889 this no longer sufficed. Maladministration in the German sphere had brought a rebellion which had ruined trade right along the coast and produced a popular hostility to Germany in London: at the same time increasing penetration of the hinterland opened up the thorny question of delimitation here too. There is no reason to believe that Salisbury regarded the area as having any great value in itself—certainly the amount of trade that McKinnon's company did was not worth a quarrel with Germany—and up to 1890 he only showed firmness when the personal position of the Sultan was affected, since the India Office set great store by his independence. But the trouble was that the rival companies stirred up public interest in exploitation as a means to obtain governmental backing, and so threatened at any moment to produce a first class row: in view of the position in the Mediterranean this could be disastrous.

[1] Salisbury to Paget 16 October 1888, in Cecil, IV, p. 112.

The second aspect derived directly from the position in Egypt. The Franco-Russian pressure on the Sultan in 1887 to reject Salisbury's terms for evacuation—terms which had included the right of re-entry in the event of civil disorder in Egypt—made evacuation impossible. Baring was quite convinced of this by 1889, since in his view withdrawal would lead to almost immediate anarchy either from Dervish pressure or from internal revolt:

> The argument based on danger from the dervishes is an excellent working argument; but it does not in reality constitute the real reason why the evacuation policy is well nigh impossible of execution. The main argument—which it is difficult to use—is based on the utter incapacity of the ruling classes in this country.[1]

To make things worse there was a strong probability that if British troops were withdrawn others might move in. The increase of Russian influence at Constantinople in this period was marked, reducing the Sultan's foreign policy to 'intermittent fits of fear—caused chiefly by the Russian Czar and our own naval power'. By 1889 there was a general expectation that something would happen 'in the spring', certainly Salisbury was sufficiently convinced to send out Hoskins, the Mediterranean C-in-C, to investigate the chances of the rumoured forthcoming descent upon Constantinople:

> There is a very prevalent idea that towards the close of the year or the beginning of next the Russians may attempt something of the kind.[2]

In these circumstances the time was not exactly propitious to proceed with evacuation, which would now have to wait, as Salisbury put it, until 'a little further on in the history of Europe'. But this decision had considerable repercussions. Now, more than ever, it was necessary to maintain good relations with the Triple Alliance powers since, in the face of French hostility,

[1] Baring to Salisbury 15 June 1889, ibid., p. 138. For a discussion of Salisbury's attitude towards evacuation see Robinson and Gallacher, p. 254 et seq.

[2] White to Salisbury 30 December 1888, Salisbury to White 9 July 1889, S.P.

Egypt was ungovernable without their support.[1] This was a new departure for Salisbury. In so far as he had any sympathies in Europe it was with France and one of the basic ideas behind his activities in 1887 had been to get out of Egypt in order to resurrect the old *entente cordiale*. Now instead he could look forward to a long term conflict with her, not only in the Mediterranean but all over the world, a prospect which was not inviting, since it meant that if relations got *too* bad he would become more than ever dependent upon Germany as the only means of keeping the 'hungry powers' at bay. But there was more to it than this. The decision to stay in Egypt, at least for the present, meant that Salisbury had to take another look at the Nile Valley. In 1884–5 the Upper Nile provinces of Egypt had been lightly abandoned: if occupation was only temporary there was little point in risking a repetition of the disasters that had afflicted Gladstone and Granville; hence the casual way in which Massowa had been offered to the Italians. But if this were not so then, ultimately, these provinces would have to be reconquered, since apart from public pressure in Egypt—which meant something to Baring—there was the danger of a European power establishing itself there.

By 1890 Salisbury had decided on reconquest but for the present lacked the means. Hence his preferred policy was to maintain the Dervishes, who were in his eyes the ideal tenants. But increasingly this became impossible as, apart from the Italians encroaching from Massowa, there were the Germans moving into Uganda. Of the two the Germans were the more dangerous. It is not clear whether even at this stage Salisbury envisaged Uganda as the jumping-off point for the reconquest of the Sudan—as he certainly did by 1892—but even if not the Germans would be a nuisance. As Baring never tired of saying, 'Egypt is the Nile and the Nile is Egypt' and German control of its headwaters could be dangerous. Not that it was so very likely that they would proceed to build a dam—a project which caught the popular imagination at this time and was much favoured by the French—but that the mere threat that they might do so would give them far too much power. Already Salisbury found that dependence upon German support in Egypt and at Constantinople circumscribed British foreign policy: how much

[1] Salisbury to Lyons 6 May 1887, in Cecil, IV, p. 45.

more so if Berlin added this weapon to its armoury! Salisbury's priorities in this situation were quite clear: with the announcement of the arrival of Karl Peters, the ex-Chairman of the German East Africa Company, in Uganda in March 1890 it became essential to reach an African settlement with Germany. Despite the current public clamour in England for the 'all red route', these dreams would be sacrificed if necessary to the exigencies of the situation in Europe. Otherwise, as Salisbury explained to the Queen in June when justifying his settlement, there would have to be drastic changes in British foreign policy:

> Under this arrangement the whole of the country outside the confines of Abyssinia and Gallaland will be under British influence up to Khartoum, so far as any European competitor is concerned . . . and any indefinite postponement of a settlement in Africa would render it very difficult to maintain terms of amity with Germany, and would force us to change our system of alliances in Europe. The alliance of France instead of the alliance of Germany must necessarily involve the early evacuation of Egypt under very unfavourable conditions.[1]

Fortunately for Salisbury the German interest in a settlement in Africa was even more pressing.

Whatever Bismarck's inclinations may have been—and as usual they were contradictory—for his successors in control of German foreign policy the German map of Africa lay firmly in Europe. Bismarck in 1888-9, whilst trying with one hand for an alliance and suggesting an African settlement, had not been averse to sharp complaints of British conduct in Zanzibar, and certainly made Munster afraid that he was about to repeat the tactics of 1884. This, Munster thought, would be fatal and he for one hailed the fall of Bismarck with relief and urged the new régime to seize the opportunity to repair the damage done in 1884 and reach a general agreement with England. This, after Bismarck's resignation, was preaching to the converted. There was a general feeling amongst those most responsible for German foreign policy—the Emperor, Caprivi, Marschall and Holstein —that Bismarck's double dealing had been too complicated and

---

[1] Salisbury to the Queen 10 June 1890, *Letters*, I, p. 613. For Anglo-German rivalry in East Africa see Cecil, IV, pp. 234-9, 278-89; Robinson and Gallacher, pp. 293-300.

dangerous. They wished to revert to a policy of 'honesty' by which they meant solidarity with Austria. In their eagerness to remove any cause for doubt in Vienna and London as to where German loyalty really lay, they now hastened to drop the Re-Insurance Treaty with Russia as too compromising, blithely oblivious of the fact that this would in turn create doubts as to German intentions in St. Petersburg. Obviously this move also had its seamy side: Waldersee looked upon 'dropping the pilot' and the Russian agreement as the first steps in his route to the Chancery and a 'preventive' war: Holstein saw it as the only means to avoid Bismarck blackmailing his way back to power. But whatever the motives behind this 'New Course' they all added up to the same conclusion, the necessity of an alliance with England.

If Germany was to decide firmly in favour of Austria—and it can be argued that this was done for the first time in 1890—then the value of the Mediterranean alliance was enhanced. Since also Crispi chose this time to put in a bid for Tripoli and raise trouble over Tunis, and apply to Berlin for British support, there was all the more urgency to reach agreement over East Africa. As Holstein put it, 'we rate our European relations higher than our colonial interests'.[1] Caprivi himself, always lukewarm where Africa was concerned, made quite clear to his ally in Vienna where the point of this new agreement lay:

> General Caprivi was a firm adherent of the moderate principles
> of the Triple Alliance and had expressed himself most enthu-
> siastically as to the results to be anticipated from the German
> arrangement with England and the British support of the
> Triple Alliance.[2]

Not all German officials were of this persuasion, in particular those most closely concerned with colonial affairs strongly opposed Salisbury's claims, but the views of the Emperor were decisive. In his case Salisbury's offer of Heligoland in exchange for a favourable settlement ended the debate: 'in comparison our East African interests merely come forward as matters for con-cession'. Suffering from one of his recurrent bouts of Anglomania

[1] *Holstein Papers*, III, pp. 340–2, 346, 352–3, 374; Ritter, pp. 21–22; Nichols, *Germany after Bismarck*, pp. 50–64.

[2] Paget (quoting Kálnoky) to Salisbury 25 September 1890, F.O., 64/1233, No. 254.

—Malet reported that 'his drift is strongly towards England and away from Russia'—the dream of naval grandeur that possession of Heligoland opened up made an African empire small beer in comparison.[1] Besides, since all the emphasis was upon collaboration with England what was the point of quarrelling with her over Africa?

From the German viewpoint then, quite obviously, this agreement was but the prelude to a closer relationship between England and the Triple Alliance. By concessions to England in Africa they hoped to create the necessary confidence to obtain what the logic of the 'New Course' demanded: reliable British support for Austria and Italy in the Mediterranean. Various attempts to obtain this were made in the course of the next two years, without very much success, until the return of Gladstone in August 1892 made it obvious that closer ties were impossible. That these attempts failed was due to a variety of circumstances; partly Salisbury's continuing internal difficulties; partly the growing spectre of the Franco-Russian alliance, particularly after the French visit to Cronstadt; but most of all because Salisbury's view of the Heligoland agreement was very different from that of Berlin. To Salisbury this had been a means of continuing an existing relationship, not of developing a new one: the present system fitted in tolerably well with the Government's position at home, whilst catering admirably for British requirements in the Mediterranean. Any more definite alliance would not only prejudice the position of the administration, but would also embitter relations with France to no particular purpose. This was a difference of standpoint which, naturally, Berlin and Rome were very slow to appreciate, partly because the new men (Crispi also fell in January 1891) took time to understand the position which had baffled even Bismarck.

If it was then primarily European considerations which determined the German agreement with England on Africa in 1890, it is not surprising that the Triple Alliance powers were disappointed with the long term results. None so more than Italy. Since 1887 Crispi had been using the German alliance in Africa, as in the Mediterranean, to persuade England to make him concessions. By this method he had made several fruitless

[1] Malet to Salisbury 18 May 1889, 22 July 1890, F.O., 343/10, 12. G.P., VIII, Nos. 1680–81.

stabs at Zeila, and obtained, with more success, British benevolence in Abyssinia and grudging acceptance at Zanzibar. As a
result of this and other factors, by the end of 1889 Italy had
emerged as the predominant colonial power on the north-east
corner of Africa, with claims that stretched from the Nile to the
Indian Ocean. Contrary to general expectation in Italy, this
domination of Abyssinia had evoked no protest from London.
Despite the Hewitt Treaty of 1885 Salisbury had no compunc-
tion in abandoning Abyssinia to Italian civilising influence. In
May 1887 he gave what assistance he could to Rome in blockading the Red Sea coast to stop arms getting to the Abyssinians,
even making some territorial concessions over the heads of
protests from Kitchener; in December he sent off Portal on a
fruitless journey to Adowa to persuade the Negus John to accept
Italian terms; in 1889 he accepted without demur the Italian
announcement of a virtual protectorate over Abyssinia, despite
the fact that Baring was becoming slightly restive. The explanation was simple, as he put it rather illogically to the India Office
when they questioned his policy of making a free gift of the
country to Italy:

> The Abyssinians have behaved very badly to us and have no
> claim on us after their treatment of Portal. On the other hand
> the alliance with Italy is a matter of Imperial policy.[1]

As long as Italy confined her attentions to regions which had no
particular interest for Salisbury this continued to be true but
when, in 1890, their attention turned to the Sudan then the
argument of Imperial policy no longer applied: now they were
infringing a direct Imperial interest, what Harcourt was later to
call 'den freien Britischen Nile'.

Crispi's motives in seeking to expand into the Sudan in 1890
were the usual mixture of grandiose and impractical ideas with
immediate and solid gain. Kassala, the richest of the Sudan
provinces would, if acquired, at last make Massowa an economic
proposition instead of a drain on the Italian State; a campaign
in this direction would pacify the military who were continually
advocating this as the solution to the frontier problem; last, but

[1] Minute by Salisbury on India Office letter 26 September 1888, F.O.,
78/4169; Salisbury to Malet 16 November 1887, S.P.; G.P., IV, No. 909;
Crispi, *Guerra d'Africa*, p. 163; Conti-Rossini, pp. 1–11.

not least, it would reopen the perspectives which had first induced Mancini's interest in this region in 1885, an Anglo-Italian alliance in Africa. Crispi had always regretted the Italian rejection of the invitation to participate in the occupation of Egypt in 1882 and from 1887 onwards had continually urged upon Salisbury that the invitation should be renewed. Now, with the campaign in Abyssinia over, he thought the time had come for a joint Anglo-Italian reconquest of the Sudan as the initial step in a new Dual Control.[1]

But unfortunately for Crispi's hopes, and to his utter incomprehension, Salisbury did not wish to share the government of Egypt with Italy: never keen on Dual Control at the best of times he had learnt his lesson in 1879–80 and promptly refused all the offers of assistance that flowed in from 1887 onwards. Italian support in Egypt was useful, but Italian participation in the government would be intolerable, if only because it would make the French more unmanageable than ever. This, not surprisingly, Crispi could never see. Nor did Salisbury and Baring want Italian help against the Dervishes to reconquer the Sudan. For the present neither England nor Egypt were ready to undertake this whilst once the Italians got a foothold there it would be difficult to get them out. Baring at least was quite outspoken. He had no doubts of the friendly intentions of the Italian Government or as to the sincerity of Crispi himself but he had no desire to see them in the Sudan, since once there, whatever their intentions, they would inevitably drift into military conquest of the province:

> I have no hesitation in saying that I should prefer to see the Dervishes in possession of Kassala and Khartoum rather than that those places should be held by the Italians . . . since so long as the Dervishes hold (them) the Egyptian Government or Her Majesty's Government . . . can choose its own time for a forward movement. But if once the Italians are in possession the case is very different.[2]

---

[1] *Guerra d'Africa*, pp. v, 2–3, 198–231; Crispi to Tornielli 17 October 1890, in *Negoziati di Napoli*; Salisbury to Lumley 28 October 1887, S.P.; Salisbury to Dufferin 9 September, 30 October 1889, F.O., 170/416, No. 202;/417, No. 233: Dufferin to Salisbury 9 March 1890, in Lyall, *Life of Dufferin*, p. 496.

[2] Baring to Salisbury 15 March 1890, quoted in F.O. Memo. 9 October, F.O., 170/432; Shibeika, *British Policy in the Sudan*, pp. 322–5.

Consequently the negotiations to settle Italian colonial claims, pursued in London, Cairo and eventually at Naples in September 1890, were a complete failure. Crispi always assumed that this was due to the influence of Baring, but in this he was wide of the mark. It was true that Cairo wished to make no concessions at all to the Italians and that in comparison Salisbury was relatively liberal. But Salisbury was only willing to concede part of the Red Sea coastal strip where, he maintained, only the magnifying glass of military strategy could discover a British interest. In the interior where the approaches to the Nile along the Atbara were concerned he was adamant, as his instructions to Baring on the eve of the Naples Conference showed:

> That we should insist upon the command of all the affluents of the Nile so far as Egypt formerly possessed them is agreed. I think you also agreed that we have no such well defined and imperative interests to safeguard on the Red Sea slope. . . I do not think that England will lose by delay. Italy is pursuing a policy which is financially impossible. . . . A good deal of exaggerated language is used in diplomatic conversation and post prandial oratory as to the value of the Italian alliance to England. . . . It is desirable: but it is not worth a very great price even in African square miles. We are negotiating in these African matters with somewhat greater ease now that we have agreed with Germany and France.

At the Naples Conference Baring and Dufferin stuck to this brief that the Sudan was an Egyptian province temporarily evacuated, which meant that Italian penetration could only be accomplished with Egyptian consent. Since Crispi refused to accept this, on 10 October Salisbury ordered that negotiations be broken off until Egyptian rights were recognised.[1]

Since, in contrast to his attitude towards Germany, Salisbury set no great value upon the Italian alliance, there was not the slightest chance of his prejudicing control of the Nile Valley on their behalf and the only result of Crispi's insistence upon Italian freedom of action was that British enthusiasm for the Italian connection waned even further. This was what Tornielli

---

[1] Salisbury to Baring 31 August 1890, S.P.; Dufferin to Salisbury, Salisbury to Dufferin, 7, 10 October 1890, F.O., 78/4325; Cecil, IV, pp. 325-9.

and Hatzfeldt had dreaded since the Kassala affair began, that Crispi in pursuing this secondary interest would forget the primary purpose of Italian policy, the maintenance of the Mediterranean alliance. Consequently when, in October, Crispi took up the idea that the military had long pressed upon him—a *fait accompli*—and announced that the seizure of Kassala was imminent, Tornielli urged the suicidal folly of such a course in view of the known feelings in London:

> If, as I believe, common interests of prime importance link our policy to that of Great Britain, if we want . . . the idea to grow here that Italy is her natural ally, we must move extremely carefully, lest we should create the least suspicion of challenging British supremacy in the Nile valley. If England should turn against us France would lose no time in profiting by it and they must know already that London is far less intransigent in the Mediterranean than Rome.

In this appraisal Tornielli was quite correct: both the London Press and Salisbury reacted strongly to the suggestion of an advance into the Sudan. Salisbury informed him bluntly that he now regretted ever favouring Italian expansion in Africa, whilst in private he began to think of reconsidering acceptance of the Italian position in Abyssinia. Whether, as Tornielli feared, he would have gone so far as to retaliate by dropping the agreement to support Italy in the Mediterranean is another question, but a fair indication of the way his mind was moving was given by the attitude that he adopted in the Bizerta question at this time. However, Crispi, whilst still considering whether to go ahead despite London, fell from office on a domestic issue leaving the Kassala dispute still unresolved.[1]

Crispi's failure to obtain any concessions in the Sudan was partly due to the fact that in this question he received no support from Berlin. The Germans now, as later, could see little point in Italian activity in this quarter which was certainly outside the scope of the Triple Alliance and far preferred to concentrate on the Mediterranean. Here, they thought, it would be possible to use the existing harmony in Anglo-German relations in the

---

[1] Crispi to Tornielli, Tornielli to Crispi, 17, 23 October 1890, A.S.C., *Carte Pisani-Dossi*, 18; Salisbury to Bertie 11 November, to Dufferin 12 November 1890, F.O., 78/4325, 170/432, Tel. 56; G.P., VIII, No. 1972.

current dispute over Tunis and Bizerta to push Salisbury forward into a more positive stand against France to the benefit of the alliance in general. Although there was some element of genuine concern in Rome at the possible fortification of Bizerta and the effect this would have upon the naval position in the Mediterranean, the way in which this was exploited in 1890 leaves little doubt that to Crispi this was just another means of getting Tripoli. Protests at London and Berlin from 1888 onwards had revealed that Salisbury had little interest and certainly would not act until the French actually showed some signs of doing something, instead of talking about it. In any case, as he pointed out,

> He could not see why Italy felt herself menaced by Bizerta when Toulon and Corsica were much nearer.

In these circumstances the rumours of Anglo-French negotiations over Tunis and of French intrigues to annexe the province on the death of the current ruler that reached Rome in June and July 1890 were heaven sent for Crispi: now he had a concrete case for 'compensation', which could only be in Tripoli. Whilst making energetic protests at London and Berlin, demanding their support on the grounds that this was an infringement of the *status quo* and therefore covered by the Mediterranean Agreement and the Triple Alliance, he nevertheless made it clear that he would not be averse to accepting compensation instead. At the same time he opened negotiations with Paris, on the grounds of Ferry's 'offer' of Tripoli in 1884, and so managed to convey to Berlin that he was thinking of changing alliances. As Ressman, Italian Chargé at Paris and a confidant of Crispi, put it:

> Crispi thinks that his countrymen might be more reconciled to the continued protectorate of France at Tunis . . . if he could obtain for them a compensating position at Tripoli. . . .[1]

At Berlin the original Italian protests over Bizerta and Tunis had cut little ice. Caprivi, quite rightly, perceived that Bizerta was a good stick to hold over Italy which helped to bind her to

---

[1] *Politica Estera*, pp. 359–64, 377–9; Gorrini, *Tunisi e Bizerta*, pp. 11–13; Memo. 7 December 1890, Dal Verme, *Bizerta* in A.S.C., *Carte Pisani-Dossi*, 15; Dufferin to Salisbury 18 July 1890, Minuted by Currie, 'I expect the meaning of this is that the Italians want Tripoli', F.O., 45/648, Tel. 41; Lytton to Salisbury 27 September 1890, S.P.

the alliance and he had not the slightest intention of regarding this as a cause for war:

> A war with France caused by this question of Tunis opens up in my opinion a much more doubtful perspective than the break up of our alliance with Italy.

But, particularly when the news came in of Crispi's negotiations with Paris, he thought it worth while to make some effort to satisfy him since the last thing that he and Holstein could afford was the loss of the Italian alliance within three months of dropping the Russians: this would give the Bismarcks much too good an opening. If not prepared to do anything active themselves they could always use England where, Caprivi was convinced, they must take Bizerta seriously: Salisbury's apparent disinterest must be diplomatic, based on the supposition that he could safely leave opposition to French schemes in the Mediterranean to Italy and Germany. Now was the moment then to press him into a more forward role and on 1 August Holstein urged upon London that they should make an immediate counter-offer in order to keep Crispi from leaving the alliance: 'the game is now in Salisbury's hands'.[1]

But Salisbury was not eager to have it. Knowing full well that Crispi's assertions about his own negotiations with the French were unfounded, and suspecting that the same was true of the supposed French negotiations with the Bey, he regarded the whole affair as just another storm in a teacup. In any case, as he told Hatzfeldt,

> The British democrats would under no circumstances allow him to take part in a war provoked by reason of the alleged treaty regarding Tunis.

The fact that Crispi did not want a war and was only using this as a lever to obtain Tripoli was slight consolation to Salisbury. He had no doubt that any sort of written offer of Tripoli to Italy would soon find its way to Constantinople, where, coming after a long series of Turco-Italian incidents, the Sultan would see in it confirmation of his current suspicion that among the European powers Russia was the one 'that will despoil him least'. Any sort

[1] G.P., VIII, Nos. 1862–3, 1872, 1888–90; *Holstein Papers*, III, pp. 348–51.

of gift of Tripoli to Crispi would, as the Germans equally realised, set off the hydra-headed Eastern Question as it would quite likely provoke a general scramble for the Ottoman inheritance.

This was one reason why Salisbury was reluctant to do anything about Bizerta, since it was all too likely that the French would promptly buy off Italian opposition by the gift of Tripoli and so spark off the powder train. But there was a simpler reason too. Despite Caprivi's assumptions, the Admiralty were genuinely unconcerned. A fortified harbour at Bizerta would possess a certain nuisance value in a *guerre de course* but this was outweighed in Admiralty eyes by its positive merit in eating up the French naval budget and dividing the French Mediterranean Fleet, making it easier to defeat in detail. Consequently the only reason for doing anything that Salisbury could see was to content 'my German friends', just in case Crispi should get something out of Paris and try to cash it. As far as Crispi's leaving the Triple Alliance was concerned Salisbury, and Dufferin, thought this most unlikely, due to alarmist reports from the German Embassy in Rome: now that 'Achitopel' had gone faith in German judgment was declining.

> I do not share these fears of the German Government. I believe that Crispi discerns them, and is bluffing in consequence; and that he hopes to take advantage of this opportunity to extract from Germany, Austria and England, a written guarantee that he shall some day be the heir of Tripoli. This written guarantee I would not be a party to giving.[1]

Salisbury's judgment in this was borne out by what followed. At the end of July Crispi sent Catalani to him on one of his confidential missions, with a personal letter explaining that French action in Tripoli was imminent and could only be prevented 'by forestalling her in taking possession of that country'. This, Crispi assured Salisbury, 'is a question of our salvation and of your supremacy in the Mediterranean'. In reply Salisbury was deliberately non-commital, carefully avoiding anything which could be construed as a *written* promise of

---

[1] Marder, pp. 150–2; G.P., VIII, Nos. 1864, 1874, 1877; D.D.F., VIII, No. 101; Salisbury to Dufferin, 26 July 1890, F.O., 170/431, No. 185A; ibid., 12 August 1890, in Cecil, IV, pp. 374–5; Hamilton to Salisbury 28 January 1891, S.P.

the province in question, limiting himself to an acknowledgment that their mutual political interests 'cannot allow Tripoli to share the fate of Tunis', whilst urging Crispi 'to avoid most carefully all action, which might compromise us irrevocably with the Sultan'. Whilst thus limiting himself on paper, in conversation, according to Catalani, he went a good deal further, expressing his conviction that:

> . . . on the day when the *status quo* in the Mediterranean shall suffer any alteration whatsoever, Italy's occupation of Tripoli will become an absolute necessity.

This dual approach provided the perfect solution to the problem. Crispi immediately announced that he was perfectly satisfied by the written and verbal assurances he had received, whilst Salisbury's letter was almost innocuous enough to be circulated to the Porte: German fears were allayed when Crispi informed them jubilantly that there was no longer any need to press for the explicit inclusion of Tripoli within the agreements with England, since Salisbury had now recognised that sooner or later this must fall into Italian hands.[1]

The major difference between London, Berlin and Rome on this issue lay in the timing of this event. Clearly both the German powers and England preferred to avoid anything likely to offend the Sultan or break up his empire prematurely. But Crispi did not share this view. Since 1887 he had been engaged in a running battle with the Porte over a series of petty incidents, occasioned really by the obvious way in which the Turks made it clear that they thought Italy of no account. Crispi himself thought the Turks had long outlived their usefulness, supported the Cretan revolt in 1889, and, despite warning from Vienna, made it quite clear that he 'had little concern for Turkish feelings but only for Italian interests'. Consequently his main idea, once he had obtained what he regarded as a guarantee of Tripoli from Salisbury, was to precipitate this happy event.[2]

The manner in which he set about this was ingenious. Italian relations with France had improved in 1890 and negotiations

[1] *Politica Estera*, pp. 367–74; Cecil, IV, 372–3; G.P., VIII, No. 1896.

[2] Crispi to Nigra, Nigra to Crispi 13, 14, 15, 16 January 1890, A.S.C., *Carte Crispi*, 161/7; Salisbury to White 10 May 1889, S.P.; Salisbury to Dufferin 8 May, 10 August 1889, F.O., 170/415, No. 94; 416, Tel. 29; Dering to Salisbury 1 October 1889, F.O., 45/625, No. 204.

had even been resumed to put an end to the economic war. This had been visible throughout the period of his agitation over Bizerta and Tunis since, both through official and unofficial channels, he had been at pains to make it clear to Paris that what he really wanted was compensation. Now that he had Salisbury's 'offer' he revealed this to Ribot and suggested that as the French contribution to a *détente* they should either use their influence at Constantinople to persuade the Sultan to part with Tripoli or they should themselves annexe Tunis. This of course, since it involved a change in the *status quo*, would enable him to cash Salisbury's cheque. But, as Ribot pointed out, this was to put too high a price on a mere improvement of relations: to obtain this Italy would first have to leave the Triple Alliance, since the Sultan would certainly not part with Tripoli without a war. Instead, suspicious of Crispi's motives in urging him to annexe Tunis, Ribot consulted Salisbury and when the latter, on rather equivocal grounds, denied that any sort of offer had been made, and urged that above all France should leave Tunis alone, Ribot now made it clear that he had no intention of acting as Crispi's stalking horse and dropped the negotiations.[1]

So far then German tactics in the search to implement the Heligoland agreement by pushing Salisbury into a more forward position in the Mediterranean had met with little success. Certainly, by intervention at London, they had achieved some measure of satisfaction for Crispi in Tripoli and so prevented the possible break up of the alliance. But the assumption that this was at all likely was in any case very doubtful and the combination of Salisbury's evasiveness with Ribot's caution prevented Crispi from actually obtaining his 'compensation'. Hence his irritation in the autumn and a new round of protests to London and Berlin at supposed French intentions at Bizerta, to which was now added her designs on the Tripolitanian hinterland. These designs which, according to an Italian War Office memorandum, had been given free rein by the Anglo-French agreement of 5 August, aimed at cutting off Tripoli from Central Africa, pushing French control from Algeria to the Egyptian frontier, and so robbing the Italian heritage of much

[1] Billot, pp. 163–5; *Politica Estera*, pp. 359 et. seq.; D.D.F., VIII, Nos. 35, 163; Salisbury to Lytton 23 September 1890, in Cecil, IV, pp. 375–6; Lytton to Salisbury 27 September 1890, S.P.

of its value. But whilst there was much in this contention as far as possibilities were concerned, they caused little concern in London. Salisbury, always inclined to think that much of the colonial disputes of the time came from looking at small scale maps, was willing to follow his German friends to the extent of suggesting to the Turks that they exercise more vigilance against French encroachments on the borders of Tripoli, but he absolutely refused to make formal representations in Paris. As he explained, when pressed by Rome and Berlin in January 1891 on Bizerta, these issues were not sufficiently important to England for him to be willing to go to the length of war and consequently he saw no point in making representations which he was not prepared to follow up, and which would only cause unnecessary friction with the French.[1]

To Crispi this 'tendency in the English cabinet to make concessions to France at the expense of Italian interests', was a cause of legitimate complaint and his failure to acquire anything positive from the English alliance, either in the Mediterranean or in East Africa, was a source of intense annoyance, especially as he had a General Election in the offing. After the failure of the Naples Conference he voiced this in London, professing to be hurt that when England had made concessions to both Germany and France it had not been possible to reach agreement with 'a power so friendly to us as Italy'. Similarly even Tornielli, though much more aware of the realities of British policy than Crispi, admitted his complete inability to understand Salisbury's attitude on the Kassala, Bizerta and other questions:

> Lord Salisbury is wrong to treat Italy with such disdain. I grant you that British support for Italy is valuable, but surely it means something for England to be able to count on Italian friendship. But what benefit does Italy derive from the 'close connection' with England when the latter never supports her?

This was a fundamental misunderstanding of the situation as seen from London. Agreement with Germany had been necessary because her support was almost essential to Imperial interests in the Mediterranean: agreement with Germany was

---

[1] *Questioni Internazionali*, p. 38; Cecil, IV, pp. 377–8; G.P., VIII, Nos. 1898–900; Salisbury to Dufferin 30 January, 6 February 1891, F.O., 170/446, Nos. 26, 32.

possible because she accepted the dogma of British supremacy in the Nile valley. Similarly the agreement with France on compensation for Zanzibar, which was in a comparatively minor key, was necessary to avoid creating an additional source of controversy to add to that of Egypt, whilst easy to accomplish since it largely took the form of the cession by Salisbury of 'light land' in the Sahara in which he had no interest. What might have given Crispi real cause for alarm and complaint, a proposal to clear up Anglo-French relations on the Heligoland Treaty pattern by mutual concessions in Egypt and Tunis, was dropped on both sides as not practical politics.[1]

But neither of the considerations which necessitated concessions to both Germany and France applied in the case of Italy. As an ally in the Mediterranean she was of doubtful utility to England, an unfortunate corollary, in Salisbury's view, of the German alliance. Her fleet was regarded as unreliable whilst her hostility towards France was a dangerous embarrassment. To humour his German friends Salisbury was willing to go some way to accommodate Crispi, as his guarded gift of Tripoli indicated; but not if this would ruin relations with France, as the Bizerta question threatened to do. But in East Africa the case was very different. Here there was no German pressure to contend with after the Heligoland Agreement whilst Crispi, in claiming part of the Sudan, was threatening British supremacy in the Nile valley, the issue which was one of the key questions in British foreign policy in the 1890's. In these circumstances Salisbury could see no reason for concession; there was no urgency for an agreement with Rome, sooner or later Crispi's African policy would have to be dropped as too expensive: in the meantime on this, as on the Bizerta issue, they could be put off with fair words:

> There is a misapprehension in the Italian way of looking at affairs which causes infinite trouble. They imagine that their alliance is a pearl of great price which we would do well to secure: and on the strength of this belief they are constantly hinting that we should show our gratitude by large material concessions. I confess I do not take this view. To my mind the

[1] *Questioni Internazionali*, pp. 37–38; Cecil, IV, pp. 317–24; Dufferin to Salisbury 13 November 1890, S.P.; Deym to Kálnoky (quoting Tornielli) 2 February 1891, S.A.W., VIII, 110.6A–E.

Italian alliance is an unprofitable and even slightly onerous corollary on the German alliance. Germany and Austria are very useful friends as regards Turkey, Russia, Egypt and even France. *They* value the Italian alliance greatly, because it means many battalions to them: and for their sake we value it too. But, by itself, it makes our relations with France more difficult: and it is of no use anywhere else. This discrepancy of views makes us seem unreasonable in Crispi's eyes. We are not as grateful as we ought to be for the favours shown us. It is a very difficult position for us. We have to make words do as much work as can be got out of them: for it is out of the question that we should show our gratitude to the unreasonable extent they desire.[1]

[1] Salisbury to Dufferin 16 January 1891, S.P.

IV

CRONSTADT

le regulateur de notre politique n'est ni à Berlin, ni à
Vienne; il est à Londres. Nous ferons ce que l'Angleterre
voudra. . . .

Ressmann to Cambon, 1892.

UNTIL 1890 European politics had revolved around Berlin
where Bismarck, spider like, sat weaving his intricate web
of alliances, erecting his *cordon sanitaire* around France. Whilst it
is arguable that the self-contradictions inherent in his system
would have brought it down anyway in the long run, there can
be no doubt that the policies of his successors materially
hastened this process; for the direct result of the 'New Course'
was the Franco-Russian alliance. This development, Bismarck's
nightmare since the seventies, was the obvious Russian rejoinder
to the non-renewal of the Re-Insurance Treaty and the much
advertised closer German links with England in 1891. The
Franco-Russian political convention of August 1891 was, of
course, a secret, but it had been given visible form by the recep-
tion of the French Fleet at Cronstadt in July when an Imperial
Russian military band played the *Marseillaise*: to contemporary
observers this seemed conclusive. Now France had found an ally
whose supply of cannon fodder exceeded that of Germany and
Austria combined, whilst Russia, in changing to the weaker
military power, had at least acquired an ally she could control.

The most marked effect of this new power bloc was a lessening
of German influence in Europe, influence which had been
dominant in the previous decades through the Triple Alliance
and *Dreikaiserbund*. This becomes evident if one compares the
weight carried by the voice of Berlin in the Egyptian or

73

Bulgarian questions in the eighties with the corresponding importance of France and Russia in the Armenian or Far Eastern problems of the nineties. This change reflected the new distribution of power since, at least on paper, the combined military strength of France and Russia outweighed that of Germany and Austria; whilst their naval power balanced that of England and Italy, assuming that it could be brought to combine effectively. This change in the structure of European politics obviously brought many repercussions in its wake, but, of these, perhaps the most marked was the effect upon the position of Italy. In the past she had been forced to struggle to be taken at all seriously as a Great Power: now her thirty divisions threatened to be decisive, even if generally regarded as of doubtful quality. For the question now was on which side they should be employed. In 1887 Crispi had light-heartedly committed Italy to a military convention with Germany since it seemed obvious that German victory was inevitable: but from 1891 onwards this was regarded increasingly as a questionable assumption and Crispi's military convention as a dangerous liability.

Hence a marked tendency in Rome to negotiate now with both sides and, although this took ten years to bring any concrete results in the secret agreement with France in 1902, the visible signs of change in Italian policy brought more immediate benefits in other directions. To Berlin and Vienna the Franco-Russian alliance meant that it was now essential that they hang on to their ally since, doubtful though she might be, her desertion would fatally compromise their position and possibly involve them in a war on three fronts. Hence if the only way to keep Italy was to make further concessions to her, then they would make them: a situation which explains the otherwise inexplicable phenomenon that Italy, the weakest of the three powers involved, was the one who stood to gain most from the treaties of the Triple Alliance as revised between 1887 and 1891. For Italy the Franco-Russian alliance meant that it was essential to recover her freedom of manoeuvre; now her ministers could revert to the traditional and profitable practice of the Kings of Savoy, balancing between the strongest States, leaving the final choice until the last possible moment, and in the meantime obtaining the maximum of concession from both sides. There was nothing new about *sacro egoismo,* Sonnino's rallying cry in 1914: it was the only intelligent policy for a statesman to pursue.[1]

This German anxiety concerning Italian wavering directly affected their attitude towards England. Since 1888 it had become a fixed idea in Berlin to make England the fourth partner in the Triple Alliance; this had been the major idea behind the 'New Course'. Up to a point it had worked. The removal of colonial differences had created almost complete Anglo-German harmony in 1890, marred only by the activities of Crispi in East Africa and the Mediterranean. In 1891–2, as these were dropped by his successor Rudinì, relations were now perfect, 'the honeymoon of British relations with the Triple Alliance'.[2] But there was one slight difficulty, the bride had not yet managed to get the bridegroom into church. Throughout 1891 therefore, whilst making allowances for Salisbury's internal difficulties, the Germans were more insistent than ever that Italy should receive some firm guarantee of British support: otherwise, they hinted, the 'New Course' would have to be abandoned in favour of the old *Dreikaiserbund.*[3]

On the surface it seemed that German policy in 1891–2 was reasonably successful. Italy renewed the Triple Alliance, Salisbury made colonial agreements with her and even gave some guarded reassurances of British support in the Mediterranean, reassurances which gained added weight from a measure of public approval in the Press. But this was partly illusory. Salisbury deliberately stepped up the policy of friendly gestures to Italy precisely because he would not contemplate an alliance: if, in Bismarck's heyday, the Master had been unable to persuade London into such a course, it was unlikely that his pupil could succeed now that German pre-eminence had faded away. Inevitably the effect of Cronstadt upon the Cabinet was to make them more uneasy at the naval position in the Mediterranean; particularly as it became clear that the Sultan had gone

[1] Compare the terms of the 1st, 2nd and 3rd treaties of the Triple Alliance in Pribram, I. For the negotiations in 1891 see Pribram, II, pp. 94–102.

[2] Herman, *Driebund, Zweibund, England,* p. 25, 'den Honigmond des flirt anglo-triplicien'.

[3] G.P., VIII, No. 1734; Vivian to Salisbury 2 June 1892, F.O., 45/683, No. 100.

over to Russia. This in turn led to a critical re-examination of the whole basis of British interests and consequent policy in that region which, if it did not reach any decision, was hardly encouraging to an Italian or German alliance. There had always been a strong element in England, marked amongst Liberals but noticeable even in the Conservative ranks, who preferred the old *entente cordiale* and an understanding with Russia: inevitably this idea received increasing support after Cronstadt as sentiment became reinforced by common sense. This became so evident by 1892 that Tornielli, for one, was convinced that England would never join the Triple Alliance: in his view 'who builds on England builds on sand'.[1]

Hence, faced with this uncertainty as to British naval power and the views of his own colleagues, Salisbury was more unwilling than ever in 1891 to do anything liable to annoy France or Russia, a tendency which developed under Rosebery into an attempt to collaborate with them rather than with the *Triplice*. But there was another side to the situation. Salisbury, relatively unaffected by the sentimental attractions of France or Russia, could yet see merit in their alliance. If it did nothing else, it effectively broke up the *Dreikaiserbund*, that alliance of the 'three Northern Courts' which had had such an inhibiting effect upon British policy in the past. As long as St. Petersburg was estranged from Berlin then British ambitions at Constantinople and elsewhere were relatively safe. It was true that the Franco-Russian alliance had its dangers, notably that it might tempt the French into actions they would otherwise draw back from. But Salisbury seems to have been convinced, rightly, that the French would never present any danger to England whilst Germany existed and, if this were so, then the present arrangement of the European powers suited him well enough. The commitment of German policy to the defence of Austria gave England room to manoeuvre: England could now replace Germany as the power with a foot in both camps and it is in this sense that it can be said that the withdrawal of Bismarck from the scene made Salisbury the new conductor of European diplomacy.[2]

[1] G.P., VIII, No. 1735; H. P. III, No. 319; Morley, II, p. 654.
[2] Israel, p. 34; 'Mehr und mehr zeigte es, dass der Schwerpunkt der europäischen Politik nicht mehr in Berlin lag. Salisbury trat in Bismarck's Fusstapfen und übernahm die Vermittlerolle. . . .'

This conclusion on Salisbury's part led to some paradoxical results. In Crispi's time Salisbury's energies had been directed towards limiting British support to Italy lest Crispi should use it to attack France. But in 1891 the position changed. Rudinì and his successor, Brin, were obviously not bent on aggression: as Brin put it in June 1892 Italian policy was 'wholly and solely directed to the preservation of peace based on the maintenance of the status quo'.[1] Now the greater danger was that Italy, in the face of Cronstadt, and despairing of British support, would desert the Triple Alliance. This, to Salisbury's mind, had to be avoided; not so much because he would miss Italian support but because the Germans would. If their military position became impossible there was a great danger that Berlin would rebuild the line of St. Petersburg by dropping that to Vienna: with Giers reluctant to finally commit Russia to the Tsar's new ally, whose standing was embarrassed by the Panama scandals, German overtures might well be accepted. Hence in order to keep Germany away from Russia, Salisbury now bent all his energies to keeping Italy in the Triple Alliance, as long as this could be achieved without any firm commitments from England. Words therefore now had to be stretched farther than ever.

German alarm at the apparent course of Italian policy commenced with the fall of Crispi in January 1891 at a time when negotiations for the renewal of the alliance had run into difficulties. His successor, Rudinì, a Sicilian nobleman of the Right, was almost an unknown quantity outside Italy but he had the reputation of being pro-French and he had certainly been among the foremost of Crispi's critics. Not that by 1891 Crispi was regarded as any great loss: both London and Berlin were at one in welcoming his departure with relief and eventually Rudinì was recognised at his true worth, 'a gentleman, preferable to his predecessor in every respect'. But until it was clear just what his pro-French feelings were going to mean in practice, his allies were naturally reserved. Their suspicion was not altogether unfounded. Although most of the alarm was due to the fact that Crispi had built himself up as the only partisan of the German alliance in Italy, Rudinì undoubtedly wanted to improve relations with France. This for obvious enough reasons.

---

[1] Vivian to Salisbury 1 June 1892, F.O., 45/683, No. 99.

As Crispi's critics had frequently pointed out the effect of his policies had been to make Italy utterly dependent upon Berlin: what was needed was to restore at least the possibility of an opening towards Paris.[1]

The necessity of such a move was dictated by the state of Italian finances. These had got rapidly worse under Crispi's régime, largely due to increased expenditure upon armaments, with the result that the annual deficit had risen astronomically. The obvious solution—borrowing—was difficult because of the main sources of finance, the French *bourse* had been closed to Italian securities whilst German houses were reluctant to send good money after bad. Increased taxation and administrative economy, theoretical alternatives, were politically impossible if Rudinì were to survive in office; this was the issue which had brought Crispi down. Cuts in Africa would not provide enough whilst reductions in military expenditure were difficult to effect in view of the opposition of the King and the state of Europe. The main hope therefore had to be to restore the flow of capital from France, but for this some sort of political understanding was essential.[2]

Rudinì claimed that such a move was not incompatible with the Triple Alliance. As he told Bruck, the Austrian Ambassador,

> his object was to lead France to appreciate the real nature of the alliance and remove all unjust suspicions and minor asperities.

But in this, as Bruck forecast, he was somewhat optimistic. His suggestion that financial concessions from Paris should pave the way for a Franco-Italian understanding in the Mediterranean, left Ribot unmoved. With the French position in Europe rapidly improving now that German links with Russia had been broken, Ribot was out to nullify the Triple Alliance and saw no reason to throw away his best card prematurely for mere verbal assurances. With impeccable logic he suggested that if Italy's alliance with Germany were as harmless as Rudinì maintained,

[1] Hermann, pp. 20–22; Farini, *Diario*, 6 February 1891; D.D.F., VIII, Nos. 247, 251; Pribram, II, pp. 94–97.

[2] *Atti Parlamentari*, 2 March, 5 May 1891; 25 May 1892; Dufferin to Salisbury 4 February 1891, F.O., 45/665, No. 18; 22 March 1891, F.O., 45/665, No. 50. Farini, *Diario*, 6 February 1891; D.D.F., VIII, No. 288.

why not publish it? Before France would make any financial concessions he wanted solid, written, guarantees that 'if we do not attack Italy she will not use the funds we have lent her to attack us'. This was exactly the sort of agreement that, ten years later, Delcassé was able to obtain, but in 1891 Rudinì and the King thought it too dangerous to pursue. Instead they insisted that Italy could only negotiate on this with the consent of her allies: Berlin, approached in March, was completely damping and any real prospect of agreement now disappeared. The negotiations with Paris continued in a desultory fashion until broken off by the French after the renewal of the Triple Alliance in June, but, as far as Rudinì was concerned, this was more to quieten his domestic opposition than anything else.[1]

The final blow to Italian hopes of an accommodation with France came from Salisbury. Rudinì seems to have had the idea, when his German allies were so unresponsive, of substituting an alliance with England. This, if it could be obtained, would give him the best of all worlds: England would protect Italy against France, Italian forces would be sufficient for self-protection against Austria, French capital would be available to balance his budget. Meanwhile the anti-Crispi groups who refused to join the Government whilst Italy remained in the Triple Alliance, would then flock to join Rudinì. That this was his object emerged in the course of negotiations over Africa. In February, somewhat alarmed at the reputed intentions of Rudinì, Salisbury had hastened to set him on the right path:

> You should express our strong approval of a pacific and friendly policy towards all foreign powers, combined with un-relaxed preparation against the dangers of war. These possibilities are so formidable that Italy cannot safely disarm. Any serious change of policy in that direction might bring on a war. Hint that if economies are wanted it might be worth while to consider what profit the African expenditure has brought or is likely to bring to Italy.

Rudinì, who had no interest whatsoever in Africa, hastened to respond to this. Accepting without discussion Tornielli's view

---

[1] Rudinì to Nigra 10 February 1891, S.A.W., XI, 106. Varia d'Italie; D.D.F., VIII, Nos. 261, 342; G.P., VII, No. 1402; Farini, *Diario*, 7 May, 20 June 1891.

that it was Crispi's campaign in the Sudan which had alienated Salisbury from Italy in the Mediterranean, he now proposed to cede all of her territory in East Africa to England,

> for a consideration which I take to be some guarantee of Italy against France. He harps frequently on the fact that he would like to get out of the Triple Alliance if he could get an alliance with England.[1]

But this did not suit the requirements of British policy. Rudinì's estimate of the situation was wrong. Certainly Crispi's forward policy in the Sudan and pressure over Bizerta had irritated Salisbury and he welcomed the change of policy in Rome: Rudinì's announcement of his intention to withdraw in East Africa, to seek good relations with France, and to drop all Crispi's disputes, earned unreserved approval in London. But this was not sufficient to induce Salisbury to an Italian alliance. All he wanted in the Sudan was to exclude Italy from the Nile: the rest of Eritrea had no particular attractions for him and in fact Italian presence there served a useful purpose in keeping the French out at no cost to England. If the British taxpayer would not pay for the reconquest of the Sudan, then there was no point in incurring the additional burden of the Italian provinces. Hence the form of the Anglo-Italian agreement of 15 April 1891 was much more limited than Rudinì had intended, providing merely Italian acceptance of the British case on Kassala, with a secret clause covering the retrocession of the Italian provinces to Egypt *if* she should ever withdraw. Of an alliance in the Mediterranean there was no mention. Salisbury had no desire that Italy should leave the Triple Alliance. Apart from the fact that an agreement to support her against France might embarrass his relations with Paris, the only result of such a policy would be an additional commitment for England with no corresponding benefit. As things were in 1891, as Salisbury told the Queen later, 'our interests lie on the side of the Triple Alliance': certainly it would be disastrous if it were to break up. Hence this invitation on Rudinì's part was quietly ignored and, instead, heavy hints dropped in Rome that as far as England

[1] Salisbury to Dufferin 8 February 1891, F.O., 170/446, Tel. 3; Dufferin to Salisbury 30 March 1891, S.P.; G.P., VIII, No. 1982; Farini, *Diario*, 2 April 1892; Conti-Rossini, pp. 53–56.

was concerned Italy would do well to renew her agreements with the German powers.[1]

The principal objection to this on Rudinì's part lay in domestic politics. Putting aside the fact that it would make the financial situation incurable—it is significant that articles providing for commercial and financial co-operation were now inserted in the treaties—it would make a stable parliamentary government impossible. With Crispi always sniping on the flank at Rudinì's 'weakness' over the Sudan and Bizerta, Rudinì's position was made untenable by the fact that his natural allies, the Piedmontese Right and the southern Left, refused to support the Triplice. But the policy they advocated—agreement with France at all cost—was suicidal, as both Rudinì and the King recognised. Hence the best that could be devised was to present the renewal of the alliance as a *fait accompli*, quickly, before the Government was overthrown, and try to make it acceptable by writing into it an agreement which would make England a fourth partner. Judging by Salisbury's hints, Rudinì assumed this would not be too difficult, especially as Crispi now informed the King that he had in his possession a written promise, apart from the 1887 agreements, of British naval assistance should the necessity arise. All that was needed, Rudinì thought, was for Salisbury to write him a similar letter that he could show to various political leaders and all his parliamentary troubles would be over.[2]

This story of Crispi's was in fact almost entirely mythical. According to the version that he told to Bruck in May 1891 this letter of Salisbury's dated from 1889 when he, Crispi,

> had applied secretly to Lord Salisbury who, without hesitation, had ordered not only that the English fleet should approach the Italian coast but that it should be powerfully reinforced.

This obviously referred to the events of July 1889 when Crispi, in one of his frequent panics, announced to Berlin and London that the French were about to attack him, in concert with an

[1] Dufferin to Salisbury 15 April 1891, F.O., 45/665, No. 65; G.P., VIII, No. 1707; Salisbury to Paget 31 March 1891, F.O., 170/446, No. 71; Salisbury to the Queen 22 August 1891, *Letters*, II, p. 65; Pribram, II, p. 96.

[2] D.D.F., VIII, Nos. 255, 342; *Farini, Diario*, 30 March, 20 June, 2 July, 1891; 13 February 1892; G.P., VIII, No. 1714; Bruck to Kálnoky 5 May 1891, 39A–K, Geheimakten XXIV/2 Rot, 463; 19 May, 43A–O ibid.

intrigue at the Vatican to persuade the Pope to leave Rome. At the time he told Solms, the German Ambassador, that Salisbury declared his solidarity with Italy, an announcement which Solms took with considerable scepticism. In fact nobody believed in this war scare except Crispi, who got it from an agent in the Vatican, and Salisbury least of all. The despatch that he sent to Rome at the time makes it quite clear that Crispi's statements were almost completely unfounded, that there was no 'extension' of the 1887 agreement:

> I said in reply that I did not at all share Crispi's apprehensions and believed the possibility of any such design on the part of France to be very small. Some phrases in the communication caused me further to add that there were no engagements between this country and Italy pledging either to material action and that I must not be understood as making any.
> However, it might be satisfactory to know that, in view of the present state of Mediterranean politics, Her Majesty's Government had resolved on strengthening the British Fleet in these waters after the Autumn manoeuvres.[1]

But Rudinì, who could find no trace of this correspondence in the archives, could only assume the story true: in which case there was nothing particularly novel in suggesting that England should be induced to join the Triple Alliance, a fact which explains the extraordinary optimism of the proposals Rudinì sent to Berlin—proposals which Hatzfeldt thought rightly, Salisbury would never accept—and the haste with which London was informed of the renewal of the alliance. On 18 May Dufferin was sent for and informed:

> that the Triple Alliance had just been renewed, then (he) recurred to his wish for a more intimate understanding between Italy and England. In the notes already exchanged between the two governments a few years back, expression was only given to their 'desires'. His ardent wish was to infuse a more positive character into the friendly relations now existing between the two countries.

Rudinì's ardent wishes turned out to be written assurances of Tripoli and naval support, both points that Crispi claimed

[1] Bruck to Kálnoky 5 May, 39A–K; Salisbury to Dering 25 July 1889 F.O., 170/416, No. 162; *Politica Estera*, p. 337 et. seq.

Salisbury had already acknowledged. Caprivi had no objection to this but when Hatzfeldt put even a watered down version of Rudinì's proposals to Salisbury he was met by a firm refusal to conclude any kind of treaty as,

> sooner or later he would have to consult his colleagues whose nervousness in such matters was known to me.[1]

The farthest Salisbury was prepared to go was to consider a rewording of the 1887 agreement to see if anything could be done to help Rudinì, but when, on 8 June, Hatzfeldt came to take this up he found that the situation had changed overnight. During the previous week Labouchère had provoked a storm in the House of Commons by taking up a story which had appeared in the French Press, and which seemed to have gained confirmation in a public statement by Rudinì, that England had joined the Triple Alliance. Rudinì of course was thinking of his parliamentary majority and assuming that he was only anticipating events: if what Crispi said was true, then Salisbury had all but done so. But the effect was to the contrary. After this publicity Salisbury was naturally chary of any commitment and fell back on the public reaction to the Labouchère debate. The Government's reply to Radical questioning was that they were at one with Italy 'in desiring the maintenance of the status quo in the Mediterranean'. From this, and the public approval which had followed, Salisbury argued that an agreement was unnecessary:

> It is clear that public opinion, in case of a French attack upon the Italian coasts, would not remain indifferent and Italy can count on British support whether or not there is any previous agreement.[2]

Since both Kálnoky and Caprivi thought it would be impolitic to press Salisbury any further at the moment, Rudinì had to rest content, on the understanding that negotiations would be taken up 'at a more favourable moment'. By this Rudinì

[1] Dufferin to Salisbury 18 May 1891, F.O., 45/667, Tel. 31; G.P., VIII, Nos. 1708–10.
[2] G.P., VIII, No. 1722; Deym to Kálnoky (quoting Salisbury) 17 June 1891, S.A.W., VIII, 110.24A–C; Cecil, IV, 380–1; Langer, *Franco-Russian Alliance*, pp. 166–7.

evidently meant after the parliamentary recess, but, unfortunately for his hopes, on 8 July the French Fleet arrived at Cronstadt and postponed the 'more favourable moment' indefinitely. Now anxious to afford visible demonstration that 'England has no antipathy to France', Salisbury invited the French Fleet to Portsmouth, whilst turning down Italian suggestions for a royal visit, on the grounds that 'it would emphasise too much England's drift towards the Triple Alliance'. To Waddington he was quite specific: whatever the Italians might say there was no naval agreement and there had been no change in British policy since 1887; a statement which was true but not exactly in accord with the spirit of his assurances to Deym and Hatzfeldt. Increasingly in the summer and autumn that followed Salisbury performed a tightrope act between his commitments to Italy and his desire to avoid antagonising the French, a performance which naturally gave rise to irritation in Rome and Berlin and finally drove Holstein to the clumsy manoeuvre of the Tuat affair.[1]

This affair, which was of no importance in itself, was the product of German alarm at the effect they thought this British indifference was having upon Rudinì. Holstein conceived that if he could get Salisbury to oppose France in Morocco then this would somehow reassure Italy and stop her drift away from Germany. This drift was real enough. Rudinì, despairing of ever renewing the negotiations at London, alarmed at the progress of the Franco-Russian alliance, now determined to negotiate direct with Russia. What he feared above all was a Continental war in which Italy was involved by virtue of the Triple Alliance but got no support from England. Hence in an effort to avoid this he met Giers at Monza on 13–14 October, asked him to use his good offices at Paris, perhaps offering some assurance that Italy would not attack France unless first attacked herself. Though the content of this interview was not known, in Berlin it was immediately assumed that Italy was about to leave the alliance, leading Holstein to his attempt at Bismarckian finesse. This was a failure, as Salisbury quickly discovered the object of the

[1] Kálnoky to Bruck 22 June, Nr. 2, S.A.W., Geheimakten XXIV/2 Rot, 463; D.D.F., VIII, No. 390; Queen Victoria, *Letters*, II, 52–53, 61, 64–65; Farini, *Diario*, 21, November 1891; G.P., VIII, Nos. 1804, 1925. Langer, *Franco-Russian Alliance*, pp. 175–206.

German manoeuvre and withdrew from the question, but it did have more useful repercussions.[1]

Recognising that the German alarm concerning Italy was genuine, that the Triple Alliance might really be in danger, and that this might have undesirable results unless checked, Salisbury decided upon action on his own account. As he wrote to Dufferin on 13 November,

> . . . Germany is very anxious that we should make love to Italy, so as to withdraw her from the illegitimate embraces of her neighbour. In this we should be wise to gratify them. It is better that Germany should be reassured by Italy by means of endearments with us, than by means of bickerings with France. . . . press the note of mutual interest, esteem, and affection, without, of course, entering into any definite engagements.

Taking Dufferin at his face value Rudinì immediately wrote to Salisbury, and from this exchange of correspondence he at last acquired at least part of what he had been after since the spring. Clearly acknowledging the influence of England upon Italian policy, Rudinì pointed out that he had been assured that England sided with the German powers:

> Sans cette certitude j'aurais peut-être hésité à renouveler l'alliance.

This was a clear enough reproach for British policy since Cronstadt and Salisbury, in his reply on 11 December went to some trouble to be reassuring, explaining his constitutional difficulties but emphasising that 'public opinion would support Italy'. This appears to have satisfied Rudinì for the present, since he never referred to the matter again, and in 1892 he went out of his way to make a demonstrative stand with England at Cairo and Constantinople during the current Egyptian disputes between England and France. Even Berlin was now satisfied of the genuineness of Salisbury's intentions: all that remained in doubt was his capacity to carry them out.[2]

This doubt was well founded. Throughout 1891 the Admiralty

[1] Bruck to Kálnoky 19, 22 October 1891, S.A.W., XI, 105.78A–B; 79A–F. D.D.F., IX, No. 32–35, 73–76; G.P., VIII, Nos. 1922–4, 1940.
[2] Salisbury to Dufferin 13 November 1891 in Cecil, IV, 383; Rudinì to Salisbury 21 November, Salisbury to Rudinì 11 December 1891, S.P.; Vivian to Salisbury 6 April 1892, F.O., 45/685, Tel. 17.

and the Cabinet had been increasingly worried by the prospect of a naval war with France and Russia. This renewed anxiety was occasioned not so much by the Cronstadt visit in itself since the probability of Franco-Russian naval co-operation had been assumed since 1888, but by the gradual realisation that despite the 1889 programme England was still inferior at sea. Until the 1889 programme had been completed this had been more or less anticipated but the cause for alarm in 1891 was the discovery that France and Russia had increased their building rate too and that, when the 1889 programme was completed, the situation would be worse than ever before. By 1891 the situation in the Mediterranean was already serious. According to Beresford the British Mediterranean Fleet of eleven battleships was both outnumbered and outclassed by the French at Toulon, whilst the Italians, on whom England was supposed to be depending, were more of a liability than an asset:

> If hostilities suddenly broke out as we are at present situated, the best plan appears to me for the British Fleet to go right through the Straits and Northwards and meet the reinforcements sent from England. This plan would however leave France absolute Mistress of the Mediterranean. . . .[1]

To make matters worse there were the Russians to be considered. Since 1890 it had become evident that the original idea of repeating the manoeuvre of 1878 in the event of war with Russia was a dead letter. The Sultan could no longer be relied upon as an ally, a fact which became even more evident after Cronstadt:

> the Orientals w(oul)d have to change their skins like the Leopard if they had not modified their views on the subject since Cronstadt. The principal subject . . . requiring constant vigilance here is the Sultan's growing disposition to adopt obligations towards Russia of strict neutrality on his part.[2]

Since the form that his neutrality took in practice was to fortify the Dardanelles whilst leaving the Bosphorous relatively unguarded, any British action aimed at preventing Russian seizure

[1] Beresford to Hoskins 10 September 1891, B.P., Add. MSS. 49713. For the general situation see Marder, pp. 150 et. seq.

[2] White to Salisbury 12 October 1891, S.P.; Langer, *Franco-Russian Alliance*, pp. 200–26.

of Constantinople would have to contemplate first forcing the Straits. By 1891 there was an added complication. At the Congress of Berlin, the Russians, not possessing a Black Sea Fleet of any importance, had insisted that the Straits be closed to all warships: England, possessing naval superiority and the Turkish alliance, had insisted that the Sultan had the right to open them if he wanted to. This now rebounded since, with a strong Black Sea Fleet and an increasing influence at Constantinople, there was now a considerable danger that the Russians would soon be able to emerge at will into the Mediterranean. Balfour, who took a great interest in defence matters and who had been in correspondence with Beresford and Hamilton, expressed the essence of the problem as it stood at the end of 1891:

> The Return . . . seems to me very clear and interesting, it is also somewhat disquieting. It would appear from it that after making all deductions and qualifications, a war against France and Russia combined might end in our losing command of the sea, and with the command of the sea, our National existence. A war with France and Russia is, I trust, a remote contingency, but the whole course of our diplomacy and the inevitable facts of the European situation compel us to regard it as a possibility, and I confess that the perusal of these Tables fills me with anxiety.
>
> The Admiralty, I understand, admit that we are not a match for these two countries at the present moment. . . . I presume that the distribution of the Russian fleet gives us an advantage not clearly shown in the tabulated statement of numbers of ships. Some of their most powerful warships built and building are shut up in the Black Sea. But it takes four years to build a first class ironclad. It might under imaginable contingencies take much less than that time to give free access to the Mediterranean of the full Russian strength now cut off at Sebastopol.[1]

The Admiralty's conclusions from this state of affairs were presented to the Cabinet as a joint report from the Naval and

[1] Balfour to Hamilton 29 December 1891, B.P., Add. MSS. 49778. The Return disclosed the following statistics:

Capital ships	First Class		Second Class	Third Class	
England	10	20	10	10	10	11
France and Russia	10	23	12	15	6	6
	Built	Built and Building				

Military Intelligence Departments in March 1892. Their conclusions were alarming. The naval advisers had always been highly reluctant to fight a war in the Mediterranean. Since 1887 Hamilton had constantly reiterated the theme that the object of naval strategy should be to post strong squadrons all around the world to cover commerce: otherwise there would be such a panic in the City on the outbreak of war that it 'might fatally hamper if not upset the strategical naval policy of the Government of the day'. He had never liked the idea of forcing the Straits and, after Hoskins's report in 1889 that the new fortifications made this increasingly hazardous, had wanted to withdraw the Mediterranean Fleet to Gibraltar, whence it could easily make a junction with the Channel Fleet. At the time Salisbury had overruled him but now, in 1892, with the joint verdict that Salisbury's intentions were impossible of execution, the Admiralty pressed for a revision of policy. In their view all thought of operations against the Straits must be abandoned since the only result would be to cripple the Mediterranean Fleet, leaving it then to be caught between the Russian and French squadrons. Once this had been accomplished England was open to invasion as the Channel Fleet alone would be too weak to oppose the French:

> The position may be summarised as follows: unless we are acting in concert with France, the road to Constantinople for a British force bent on belligerent operations, lies across the ruins of the French fleet.[1]

The only fault with this strategy of withdrawal from the Mediterranean was that it cut right across the assumptions and needs of foreign policy. Throughout 1892 the Germans warned that the British Fleet there was too weak, that their agents in Turkey were unanimous that the Sultan would not resist a Russian attack, that unless the British force was strengthened Italy would collapse at the first shot. Manifestly this was not the moment to withdraw what forces there were available: the result could only be a German agreement with Russia. But equally the situation could not be left to rot indefinitely. Salisbury's conclusion on this was quite clear: there was no absolute

---

[1] Hamilton to Salisbury (undated) 1889, 29 April 1890, S.P.; Report of D.M.I. and D.N.I. 18 March 1892, printed for the Cabinet 8 June; copy in Salisbury Papers.

urgency since it seemed that the Russians, whatever their ultimate intentions, were in no position to risk a general war at the moment. But,

> the early attention of whoever is responsible for the conduct of Foreign Affairs cannot be withheld from it without public danger for very long. For the upshot of this Report is, that the Foreign Office on the one side, and the defensive Departments on the other, have been proceeding on lines as far divergent as it is possible for lines of policy to diverge: it is evident that if this difference is maintained until the moment for action arrives nothing but the most serious disaster can be the result.

This report involved enormous changes in British foreign policy. Not only in England but also in Europe, the protection of Constantinople had been assumed to be the turning-point of British policy for more than forty years. It was the only interest in the Mediterranean worth defending and if, as it appeared, it was no longer defensible,

> our policy is a policy of false pretences. If persisted in it will involve discomfiture to all who trust in us and infinite discredit to ourselves.[1]

But for Salisbury time had run out. There was a General Election pending in which his chances of victory were 'very shadowy'. His Government was on its last legs: Smith was dying, Goschen sulking; Chamberlain and Hartington engaged in civil war; the former pressing Salisbury to adopt a radical programme on social issues which he thought 'destined to break up our party'. As he confided to Balfour, it was impossible to adopt any act of vigour just then: 'Resolute Government is only possible in Ireland.' Obviously it was impossible to take any decision of this magnitude in the field of foreign policy, since it would be bound to involve basic changes in England's scheme of alliances. Moreover, it is clear that Salisbury himself, whatever his colleagues thought, disagreed with the Admiralty conclusions. Never inclined to take 'expert opinion' too highly, he was averse to the wholesale changes that their conclusion demanded. But all that he could do was to stress the importance of the problem and leave to his successor, with a clear guide

---

[1] F.O. Memorandum in comment on Joint Paper of D.M.I. and D.N.I. 4 June 1892; Malet to Salisbury 2 March 1892, B.P., Add. MSS. 49690.

to what, in Salisbury's view, was the correct course to follow.[1]

This he gave in the 'Political Testament' which he left with Currie, the Permanent Under-Secretary at the Foreign Office, and in a letter which he wrote to the Ambassador at Berlin, Malet. The origin of this lay in Rome and Berlin. By mid-July 1892 it was evident that Gladstone had won the elections and Hatzfeldt, who, like Tornielli, was convinced that Gladstone would repudiate any agreement with Italy, reported this to Berlin. This worried the new Foreign Minister in Rome, Brin, 'especially if Labouchère gets in the Cabinet', and he appealed to Berlin for assistance. Consequently Hatzfeldt was instructed to make formal representations to Salisbury of the disastrous effects that any such Gladstonian move might bring. In an interview on 4 August Salisbury promised to do what he could, notably to pass on to Rosebery his own conviction that British relations with Italy were the key to European peace.[2]

Salisbury's views as expounded in these two letters show quite clearly what he had been trying to do for the past six years. His assurances to Italy had not been absolute because policy in England was determined by national feeling, which, in turn, hung on the nature of the cause of war. But on the other hand he had promised them to consult with Rome if the *status quo* were threatened since, with their fleet weak and their ports exposed, they were completely open to French attack. It was essential that Italy should not feel that England gave even a moral preference for France since this would wreck what Salisbury thought was the key to the present situation in Europe, 'our position towards Italy, and through Italy to the Triple Alliance'. If this were to be abandoned then dire consequences would follow for European peace and England's interests generally:

> What I am afraid of is too hurried a rapprochement with France, involving the abandonment of the Triple Alliance by Italy—a reconstruction of the Drei-Kaiser-Bund and Russia on the Bosphorous. I think the past will be sufficient to warn us against this risk.[3]

[1] Salisbury to Balfour 1 October 1891; 26 July 1892; Balfour to Salisbury 24 July 1892, B.P., Add. MSS. 49689, 49690.

[2] G.P., VIII, Nos. 1732–4; Vivian to Salisbury 29 July 1892, S.P.

[3] Salisbury to Malet 16 August, Salisbury to Currie 18 August, S.P The letter to Currie, partly printed in Cecil, IV, p. 404, was obviously intended for Rosebery's consumption.

V

THE END OF THE MEDITERRANEAN AGREEMENTS

> It would be the means of our retaining the command of
> our most important communications. In fact by taking
> Egypt absolutely, we would secure what we have sought
> to maintain by keeping Russia out of Constantinople.
>
> D.N.I., November 1895.

CONTRARY to general expectation the German fears that
the advent of the Liberals would mean the immediate end
of British association with the Triple Alliance, turned out to
have been unfounded. For the next two years Rosebery, first as
Foreign Secretary, then as Prime Minister, maintained the
relationship much as it had been in Salisbury's day: it was only
with the Congo affair in 1894 and the Armenian crisis of 1895
that there was much change in the attitude of the Liberal
Cabinet. Even so this change was not decisive: the attempt to
work with Russia failed; so that Salisbury could assure Berlin
with considerable truth in 1896 that his policy was much the
same as it had been in 1892. Why then did this relationship,
which had been fostered so carefully since 1887, break down
during 1896, to be replaced by the celebrated 'Splendid Isolation'? The answer to this is more complicated than it appears at
first sight. Partly it is a question of changing circumstances: the
Armenian massacres made it difficult to envisage defending
Turkey. Partly it was a change in the internal balance of the
British Cabinet: the opposition to Salisbury's ideas was much
greater after 1895 than it had been from 1887–92. But, more
than anything else, it was a change in attitude of mind. On the

surface relations might still seem perfectly good and differences difficult to pinpoint: but, by 1896, in Berlin they were convinced that negotiations with England were a waste of time, whilst in London there was a distinct feeling that the Triple Alliance was a broken reed.

German and Italian fears in 1892 had been based on the attitude of Gladstone, an attitude which was restated in August of that year in an open letter to the *Corriere di Napoli* emphasising his disapproval of Italy's military alliances. Moreover he was known to be 'unsound' over Egypt: even in 1892 he still talked of evacuation, a highly alarming prospect in Rome and Berlin, since such an action would remove the principal obstacle to Anglo-French understanding. Hence their relief when it became known that Rosebery had accepted the Foreign Office and that Labouchère—a likely candidate for the Under-Secretaryship—had been excluded. Now they were relatively certain that, as Caprivi assured the Austrians,

> As long as the foreign policy of England remains in the hands of this statesman, the position she has assumed in relation to the Triple Alliance will be unaltered.

This feeling was confirmed by Rosebery himself in an explicit statement of his policy on 6 September. Gladstone, so he told Hatzfeldt, was old and his dominating influence was not what it used to be:

> he, Lord Rosebery, could assure me without exaggeration that he was almost indispensable to the inherently weak Ministry, and was therefore much stronger than formerly.

This was perfectly true. With only a small majority and most of his colleagues at sixes and sevens, Gladstone's position was almost impossible. Rosebery himself made it worse by a long drawn out threat to withdraw from public life, with the result that he had to be begged to accept the Foreign Office. Consequently he was able to state his own terms, which were quite simple: an entire free hand in foreign policy, which was to be conducted with almost no reference to the Cabinet, and enforced by the constant threat of resignation. In these circumstances, however much Gladstone and Waddington might want to do something about Egypt, Rosebery had a complete veto;

and within a few months of the Liberal administration taking office Anglo-French relations were far worse than they had ever been under Salisbury. Small wonder then that Gladstone, in retrospect, regarded Rosebery's appointment as one of his greatest blunders, since the effect was to exclude himself from any influence over foreign affairs.[1]

This situation, greatly appreciated by the Queen, who dreaded entrusting her Empire to the 'old, wild and incomprehensible man of $82\frac{1}{2}$', was equally acceptable to the German powers. Rosebery's public affirmations of his support for Salisbury's foreign policy, his specific reassurances to Hatzfeldt, of which he gave written confirmation, seemed convincing enough. Even Tornielli now began to have faith, whilst Brin pointed out with perfect truth that they were almost as certain of Rosebery's support as they had ever been of Salisbury's.[2] As British relations with France and Russia got worse in 1893 with the development of the disputes over Egypt, Uganda, Siam and Afghanistan, so German and Italian confidence grew correspondingly. In May 1893 the retiring British Ambassador at Vienna made an official speech emphasising British solidarity with Austria: in June Rosebery assured the Italians that France was 'driving England into the arms of the Triple Alliance'. In July the Siam crisis broke. Now both in Rome and Berlin it was assumed that the moment had arrived: the prospect of an Anglo-French war and Rosebery's appeal to the Emperor for German assistance, convinced them that England would now join the Triple Alliance. Hence the enormous sense of disillusionment when this failed to materialise.

The effect of this crisis upon German policy was fatal for the future of the British association with the Triple Alliance. Coming after past failures to pin either Salisbury or Rosebery to a definite position, the German conclusion from Rosebery's action over Siam was that if he would not fight even when assured of German assistance, then no reliance could be placed on England.

[1] Széchényi to Kálnoky 20 August 1892, S.A.W., III, 140.90B; G.P., VIII, Nos. 1737–40; B.D., VIII, pp. 4–10; James, *Rosebery*, pp. 235 ff.

[2] Queen Victoria, *Letters*, II, pp. 141–7; G.P., VIII, Nos. 1738, 1741–2. This was Currie's view, of some importance in view of his position as Permanent Under-Secretary; Deym to Kálnoky 3 November 1892, S.A.W., VIII, 112. Brief. See the discussion in Israel, p. 46.

In point of fact they were wrong, Rosebery merely thought the issue not worth fighting over, as his letter to the Queen makes clear:

> Resort to the Triple Alliance may some day be necessary and no doubt the French are trying their best to drive us to it. But this should be in some direr strait than at present. It becomes your Majesty's dignity to settle this matter without such assistance.

But from this time onwards Berlin would no longer be content with half a loaf. It was all or nothing: either England joined the alliance or Germany would abandon the 'New Course' and reach agreement with Russia. As a result the real chance of a close agreement that emerged from Rosebery's negotiations with Austria over the Straits in 1894 was thrown away, whilst Germany embarked on the *Kolonialpolitik* which was to alienate not only Rosebery but also, more important, British public opinion.[1]

These negotiations demonstrated clearly that, whatever might be the view taken by Berlin, London and Vienna still had considerable interests in common and that Rosebery was prepared to go to remarkable lengths to preserve these. The cause of this mutual anxiety was, as usual, the Mediterranean, where both Kálnoky and Rosebery were worried at their prospects in a war with Russia. Kálnoky, already alarmed at the evident trend of German policy, was also seriously preoccupied with the state of affairs in Italy. Here the combination of social disorder and financial chaos threatened to bring down the monarchy, whilst a republic would inevitably enthrone the irredentists. If Austria were to be deserted by both her allies then she too would have to make her terms with Russia, a prospect that was so unwelcome to Kálnoky that he determined to have one last attempt to push England into a more forward role. If only Rosebery could be induced to be more warlike then this might both bolster up Italy and reverse the German drift towards Russia:

> . . . the psychological moment has come for England not only to increase her navy, but also to make up her mind whether she intends to assert her traditional political authority or whether

[1] Rosebery to the Queen 26 June 1893, Crewe, II, p. 424; G.P., VIII. Nos. 1745, 1755; Temperley and Penson, pp. 472–7; Israel, pp. 47–53.

she will allow herself to be crowded out of the Mediterranean, where British power has hitherto been predominant.[1]

For his own reasons Rosebery was in a receptive mood. The doubts which had been expressed in 1892 as to British naval power grew worse in 1893 after the Russian visit to Toulon in August. By the end of the year Spencer, the First Lord, summed up British hopes in the Mediterranean as 'a policy of bounce', since their only hope was that the Russians would be too impressed by the potential opposition to seek a decision. But with the evident weakening of the Triple Alliance it was doubtful how long this would last. The obvious solution to the problem, joining the alliance or a separate treaty with Italy, was ruled out by Rosebery: 'Neither of these, however, is in the range of practical politics for a British minister at this time.' But strengthening the fleet, which he had already determined on, was not enough. The power of the deterrent partly depended upon Austrian co-operation and Kálnoky was now threatening that unless he got a firm guarantee in writing that the Liberal Cabinet stood by the Mediterranean Agreements, then he would have to seek an understanding with Russia. Kálnoky's demand for Cabinet approval of these agreements was impossible: getting rid of Gladstone was difficult enough and, as Rosebery put it, 'il s'agît de ma tête dans cette affaire'. The Cabinet had never been consulted on this question and Rosebery had taken great care never to read the Mediterranean Agreements, so that he could profess ignorance if questioned by his colleagues. This, as he once told Deym, was the great difference between Salisbury and himself: Salisbury could at least discuss the matter in the Cabinet, he could not. But what he could do, in the light of obvious public support in England for the principle of the maintenance of British power there, was to offer a guarantee to defend Constantinople against Russia, provided that he could be assured of the assistance of the Triple Alliance to hold France in check.[2]

In Vienna this was regarded as a reasonable enough response,

[1] Memorandum by Kálnoky November 1893, S.A.W., XI, 109; Kálnoky to Deym 7 December 1893, in Langer, *Franco-Russian Alliance*, p. 368.

[2] Rosebery to Malet 3 January 1894, F.O., 363.3; Hatzfeldt to Holstein 15 February 1894, H.P., III, No. 402; Temperley and Penson, pp. 472–7, 481–7; Marder, pp. 219–20.

since Kálnoky fully realised that they could not expect a binding alliance on the Continental pattern from England and he wanted to negotiate on this basis. But Berlin was unimpressed. Caprivi had just embarked on his commercial agreement with Russia; Holstein and Kayser were preoccupied with a colonial agreement with France and intent on using their position to force colonial concessions from London and thus gain popularity at home. To call this off in return for the possible results that might flow from taking up Rosebery's gesture was unthinkable: on the contrary a little pressure in Africa 'to demonstrate the independence of our policy' might be beneficial in stimulating England, impressing St. Petersburg and pleasing the German Right. This, the origin of the Congo dispute which now followed, finished Kálnoky's hopes. The whole basis of the 'New Course' had been deferment to British colonial ambitions in return for British support in Europe and it was only logical to expect, as Rosebery pointed out to Deym on 14 June 1894, that the reversal of German policy would lead to similar action in London. When the dust had settled on the Congo dispute of June 1894 it was clear that German policy had been a mistake. That the German case was a good one was indisputable, as *The Times* never tired of pointing out. But this was immaterial. As Hatzfeldt gently suggested in December 1894, it may well have been true that nothing very much would have come of Rosebery's negotiations with Kálnoky but their continuance would have served one very useful purpose: it would have kept the British connection with the Triple Alliance alive for Salisbury's return:

> The danger here does not lie in offending some Minister or other, but in the possible shift of so-called public opinion, which is by the way already making itself felt as a result of the estrangement between us; and even Salisbury will not be able to contend with it if, by the time he returns to office, public opinion has turned decisively against the Triple Alliance.

But killing them in this manner not only alienated Rosebery, who now embarked on an attempted settlement with France and Russia, but, more important, affected public opinion, thus prejudicing the very thing Berlin was banking on.[1]

[1] G.P., VIII, No. 1850; Hermann, p. 123; Israel, pp. 62–63; Bayer, p. 103; Temperley and Penson, pp. 487–91. For the Congo dispute see, in particular, Bayer, pp. 81–95. For Hatzfeldt's views see H.P., III, Nos. 408, 430.

Increasingly after 1894 this rising popular antagonism over colonial questions, which was equally reciprocated in Germany, came to provide the background to Anglo-German relations. This naturally frightened Germany's alliance partners. Crispi, who returned to power in Rome in December 1893, immediately tried to establish an alliance with England in Africa to counter his increasing difficulties in Abyssinia. But this met with no response in London. Before the Congo affair they were willing to make a limited agreement over boundaries in the Harar, but even at this stage any attempt by Crispi to widen this to the cession of Zeila or general co-operation in the Sudan was rejected. Once the Congo dispute was under way such an agreement was out of the question: as Kimberley put it, 'We have enough on our hands without adding fuel to the fire.' At the end of 1894 Crispi, growing desperate at Rosebery's obvious tendency to work with France and Russia and afraid that this would now extend to the Red Sea, applied once more to London but without success. Hatzfeldt, enquiring on his behalf, was told that Rosebery did not want to upset his good relations with Russia which were of some importance to England, especially in view of the contiguity of the two powers in Asia; that whilst Italy could probably rely on British support in the Mediterranean, she could not expect England to share in her aggressive actions in the Red Sea, 'thereby getting into conflict with other powers'. That British policy was changing was obvious. Tornielli, who had long been harping on this theme, now trumpeted his conviction that Rosebery and Kimberley were bent on a settlement with France, and had to be removed from London to avoid embarrassment: but even Hatzfeldt regarded this as a foregone conclusion:

> For the fact remains, one may argue about it as one will, that England is now casting about elsewhere, a policy that England blames on our alienation of herself. . . .[1]

Clearly enough by the end of 1894 there was little left of the *entente à trois*. Anglo-German relations got worse with the growth of a dispute over Mozambique in which Kimberley all but

[1] Ibid., No. 430; Kimberley to Ford 8 June 1894, K.P., H.M.C. 293; G.P., VIII, No. 2004; Sanderson to Ford 5 January 1895, F.O., 170/494, No. 6.

threatened war: colonial negotiations between England and France proved abortive, but Rosebery's Guildhall speech in November and the gradual formation of the Armenian *Triplice* indicated that the new policy was to continue unabated. Kálnoky might rail at the 'third or fourth rate clerks' in Berlin who had been responsible for this, but there was no sign that Rosebery regretted the change. To judge from a letter he wrote to Malet in January 1895 he exalted in his new-found strength, seeing England now in the central position in European diplomacy:

> Gt. Britain, if her policy be properly guided, holds the key of the situation. For about five months this year Germany appeared to ignore the fact; and so I had to send her a very plain message through Vienna. Hence, too, the developments when Germany began to talk of being able to pursue a French policy in Africa, while maintaining the Triple Alliance in Europe, it was time to speak out, for they ignored the central keystone of the situation—through Italy, England. You will have observed the alarm and annoyance at Vienna and also at Rome. And now we have a very different tune at Berlin, though much harm has been done. . . .[1]

But if England was now in a position to negotiate with both sides, a position which was gradually enhanced as the effects of the 'Spencer Programme' restored her naval power, this did not necessarily entail the abandonment of her former ties: Rosebery's watchword in 1894, 'we must co-operate, but not be handcuffed to anyone', was still true in 1895. Practical co-operation as circumstances permitted rather than the hard and fast obligations of an alliance, had always been the main point of Salisbury's policy: what had changed during Rosebery's time was that it was now possible to work with Russia and France as well. This development, partly due to the change in public opinion occasioned by the colonial conflicts with Germany, partly to the Armenian massacres, created a new set of limits within which British foreign policy could operate. That Salisbury would automatically revert to the Triple Alliance was a German illusion, no more valid than their supposition that Rosebery had gone over to Russia and France. What would

[1] Rosebery to Malet 6 January 1895, F.O., 363.3; Hermann, pp. 132–5; Malet to Salisbury 7 July 1895, F.O., 363.12.

happen after Salisbury's return would depend upon circumstances, and here, as Hatzfeldt for one had long foretold, the critical issue turned out to be that of the Straits. As long as the Eastern Question was virtually confined to Armenia then it was relatively easy for England and Russia to work together; but, once the Straits question became involved, the gulf between their interests was such that co-operation became impossible and Salisbury began to seek once more to establish the old *entente à trois*.

The major question that faced Salisbury on his return to office in June 1895 was then the search for a solution to the Armenian problem. The Liberal policy of working with France and Russia to this end had, for obvious reasons, failed to produce any result since, as Salisbury quickly discovered,

> . . . there is no hope whatever of Russia consenting to apply pressure or consenting that pressure should be applied by us. What is true of Russia is true of France.

In fact Salisbury was inclined to be increasingly critical of the legacy he had inherited from Rosebery: the whole idea of reform of the Ottoman Empire and guarantees for the Armenians by the goodwill of the Sultan was ridiculous:

> Without using force to deprive the Sultan of his independent sovereignty you are imposing upon him terms which no independent sovereign would accept . . . and how are we to apply force in the absence of allies?

Just what Salisbury intended to do at this stage has been the subject of much inconclusive debate and, whilst it is a fair deduction from his remarks to Hatzfeldt about 'backing the wrong horse' that he regretted that partition had been rejected in 1853, it does not follow that he was advocating such a course in 1895. It would seem that his conversations with Hatzfeldt and the German Emperor in July were purely precautionary, to discover German views *in case* it should eventually come to partition as the only solution to the Eastern Question. Certainly he strenuously denied that he had suggested that he would give Russia Constantinople:

> I never hinted anything of the kind. I said I was sure the Germans would do it if they had a war with France.

But, whatever Salisbury's intentions may have been in July 1895, it was evident after these talks that the German powers were no keener than Russia was to become enmeshed in the Armenian issue:

> The conversations with the Austrian and German ambassadors and with the German Emperor make it quite clear (what I never doubted) that all Europe is opposed to our Armenian policy. The two German Powers certainly hate it: they think it quixotic and dangerous.[1]

In these circumstances there was little point in taking up the idea that Crispi was pressing of enlarging the Armenian *triplice* by taking in the Triple Alliance and having a grand European Conference on the pattern of 1876. The Italian idea was obvious: anything that would break up the Anglo-French-Russian group was worth trying, whilst if the Conference resulted in partition Crispi would not complain. But for Salisbury this had little attraction. His hints that Italy should begin to think of Tripoli and Albania had not been meant seriously: they were mainly intended to divert them from Zeila, where their pressure was becoming a nuisance. A conference, with Russia, Germany and Austria determined on no action, was useless:

> The only result of calling a Conference will be that we shall be politely bowed out by six Powers, instead of two, as now.

But nevertheless something had to be done. The obvious solution —and one has the impression that this was Salisbury's inclination at this stage—was to drop the Armenians: as he told Hatzfeldt later, 'my only idea is to get myself out of this nasty impasse'. But the pressure of public opinion in England made this impossible since the Armenian cause had been taken up, particularly by the Liberal Press and Gladstone, with an almost missionary zeal. It was here, really, in the Nonconformist conscience, that lay the explanation of the gulf between England and the Continental Powers, as Salisbury reflected in a letter to Currie:

> It is curious that two psychological climates can exist side by

[1] Salisbury to Currie 1 July, 12, 27 August 1895, S.P.; Minute by Salisbury on letter from Currie 2 September 1895, S.P.; G.P., X, No. 2381. See Serra, *L'intesa mediterranea*, pp. 11–12; Grenville, pp. 341–6.

side so utterly different as those of England and Continental Europe. I do not believe that from Archangel to Cadiz there is a soul who cares whether the Armenians are exterminated or not. Here the sympathy for them . . . approaches to frenzy in its intensity. . . .[1]

In these circumstances, with action at the Straits ruled out, Salisbury's solution to this problem until late September was the curious idea of landing troops at Jeddah and stirring up trouble in Arabia. It possessed the dual advantage that it would not alarm the Russians whilst it would probably impress the Sultan: its only defect was that it would have to wait until the cool weather. But before this season had arrived circumstances had changed. A renewed onslaught upon the Armenians at the end of September so horrified Europe in general that it produced a momentary spasm of unity amongst the Great Powers. Now, collectively, they enforced upon the Sultan the issue of the *iradé* of 17 October which granted all the reforms that the triple concert had been pressing for months. This had two consequences. In the first place it seemed that Russia, now, might permit the enforcement of this decree even by naval action at the Straits, with the result that for the next two months Salisbury was distracted by this red herring. In the second place, the prospect was now opened of a reformed Turkish Empire, whose defence would be acceptable to British public opinion, so permitting Salisbury to embark upon a clear-cut policy of resurrecting the former *entente à trois*. If in July he had been all gloom, anticipating the worst in his conversations with Hatzfeldt, in October he was full of optimism. He had come to the conclusion, he told Deym, that the maintenance of the Turkish Empire was the only possible policy to follow, since its break up was bound to be to England's disadvantage. He was perfectly willing to discuss the renewal of the former understanding and thought that Italy would be a willing, if not over useful, third.[2]

This news was very gratefully received in Vienna. Goluchowski, who had replaced Kálnoky in May 1895, had taken

[1] Salisbury to Currie 27 August, 17 December 1895, S.P.; G.P., X. Nos. 2371–86; H.P., III, No. 504.
[2] Salisbury to Currie 13 September 1895, S.P.; Deym to Goluchowski, 17 October 1895, S.A.W., Geheimakten XXV Karton Rot, 463.30B; H.P., III, No. 497.

Hatzfeldt's reports in July at their face value when communicated to him by Hohenlohe, and been seriously alarmed. Such great hopes had been built upon the return of Salisbury and now, it had seemed, working with England was as impossible as it had been in Rosebery's last months of office. Hence his relief in October. There was no difficulty in obtaining Italian assistance. Crispi and Blanc had been urging for months that Vienna should support the British view over Armenia and so wean her away from Russia and France. Crispi would support any action that England thought necessary: he did not care if the Empire were brought down; what was essential for Italy was that at that critical moment England should not be working with Russia and France, otherwise it was likely that Russia would emerge with Constantinople whilst Italy would not even get Tripoli.[1]

Hence the new departure in Austrian policy. Secure in the knowledge that England and Italy were once more back on the old course, on 11 November Goluchowski proposed that the powers should jointly force the Straits and actually put into effect the promised reforms of 17 October. To Goluchowski, as to Salisbury, this seemed the only way that the old policy could be made to work and thus draw England away from the dangerous collaboration with Russia. But, unfortunately for the hopes of a revived *entente à trois*, Goluchowski's interest in action was short lived. With little or no interest in the fate of the Armenians, his major concern had always been the danger of Anglo-Russian partition of the Sultan's dominions and he had seized on renewed collaboration with England to avoid this. But when, on 20 November, Lobanov made it quite clear that under no circumstances would Russia consent to the opening of the Straits, then Goluchowski rapidly retreated. To continue would, presumably, mean war with Russia, a war which was pointless from the Austrian viewpoint; since if Lobanov would not agree to the opening of the Straits then there was not the slightest chance of any Anglo-Russian deal. As Goluchowski explained when, in May 1896, Salisbury tried to educate the British elec-

[1] Currie to Salisbury 2 September 1895, S.P.; Monson to Salisbury 18 October 1895, S.P.; Eperjesy to Goluchowski 16 November 1895, S.A.W., XI, 112.69A–C.; G.P., X, Nos. 2502–9.

torate by publishing a Blue Book on the Armenian débâcle throwing the blame on Vienna,

> Austria had never had any intention of following England in a policy of adventure. Her one idea was the preservation of the harmony of action . . . Russia's explicit declaration that she must insist upon the strict observance of the Treaty of Paris in regard to the passages of the Straits made it imperative on Austria to drop the third proposal. Any insistence might, and probably would, have led to war and that for interests the importance of which to herself Austria cannot recognise. . . .[1]

This altered things considerably. Salisbury had embarked upon this revival of the Austrian alliance on the supposition that, in the circumstances of 17 October, either jointly or in concert, they would proceed to reform the Sultan and thus give his empire a new lease of life. But Lobanov's refusal to permit this and Goluchowski's withdrawal made it plain that if Salisbury were to persist it could only be by isolated British action. The evidence is not absolutely clear, but it is apparent from his correspondence with Goschen that this is what Salisbury did now contemplate. Tired of the Sultan's obstruction and Goluchowski's tergiversation he now began to regard forcing the Straits as preferable to further debate with his allies and even seemed inclined to the view that British action, if not associated with Austria and Italy, would not draw a hostile Russian response: certainly he rejected Italian offers of assistance at this time on precisely these grounds. Just what his object was in taking this action is again uncertain; he told the Admiralty that it was to forestall an expected Russian seizure of Constantinople; but just how seriously he took this it is impossible to say. More likely is that this was the excuse with which to overcome Cabinet opposition, whilst his real purpose was to establish *de facto* British control of Constantinople, enforce reform, and so save the Ottoman Empire *malgré lui*. After all, as Hamilton pointed out to Balfour, the defence of Constantinople had been one of the two major points of Salisbury's foreign policy for the last ten years and unless something drastic were done he would have to

---

[1] Monson to Salisbury 14 May 1896, F.O., 170/504, No. 156; for Austrian and Russian policy at this juncture see Langer, pp. 206–8.

write this off as a failure. Certainly Hatzfeldt was convinced that Salisbury's main object at this stage was to get rid of the present Sultan.[1]

But in advocating this idea Salisbury ran up against established Admiralty views. Doubtful even before 1892 of the feasibility of such a course, the consolidation of the Franco-Russian alliance now made it plain impossible. Since 1894, they maintained, it had been accepted that they could not act against Russia at the Straits if France were hostile too: they saw no reason to change their minds now. Sceptical of expert opinion—Salisbury held that everyone outside the Admiralty thought it easy enough—he was willing to override this opposition: in 1892, when this debate had first started, he had insisted that it was up to the Cabinet to decide, not the naval and military advisers. But the difficulty was that he could not carry his Cabinet colleagues. Goschen, now First Lord, naturally supported Richards and the naval staff in their opposition: he would only waive this if Salisbury could guarantee Austrian and Italian support or if Russian action to seize Constantinople became imminent, which he doubted. Hence his refusal to countenance the proposition which Salisbury was canvassing, that of giving Currie power to call up the fleet from Salonika at his own discretion:

> The one course to which I must object is, I fear, one which commends itself to your judgment, namely to give Currie carte blanche. As you know I am quite in accord with giving the Ambassadors jointly that discretion, but without knowing (and I don't know) what Currie would do with the fleet—what end the policy he might pursue would have in view, I cannot reconcile myself to the expediency of that step as at present advised. . . . It is a different thing to support your policy and to support Currie.

Faced with this opposition, in which Goschen apparently had the support of Chamberlain, Hamilton and Balfour, and obviously unable to produce Austrian support, Salisbury had no choice but to withdraw: as he told Goschen, 'In Armenia I

[1] Minute on Ford to Salisbury 23 November 1895, F.O., 45/735, Tel. 43; Hamilton to Balfour 12 January 1896, Add. MSS. 49778; Marder, pp. 244–8; H.P., III, No. 499.

have been told by the Cabinet practically to sit still.'[1] Thus, by the end of 1895, although no clear-cut decision had yet been taken, it seemed that all thought of a swift solution to the Armenian problem by forcing the Straits had been abandoned. Two further considerations helped to consolidate this position— the development of extreme tension with the United States over Venezuela and with Germany over the Transvaal. The serious prospect of a naval war with these two powers left little margin for risking war with Russia over the Straits.

The serious situation produced by the Kruger Telegram was a by-product of German policy in the Near East. Since July 1895 the German attitude towards the Armenian question had been clear and consistent: as Marschall told Lascelles at one stage, they preferred 200,000 Armenian dead to 100,000 German dead. Having no interest they did not intend to become involved: moreover, they would not permit their allies to become involved either. Pleas from Goluchowski and Crispi that the result would be the division of Turkey by the triple concert left Berlin un-moved: they did not believe that England and Russia could come to an agreement and, even if they did, Holstein for one doubted whether the irruption of Russia into the Mediterranean would be disastrous for Germany. Hence the pressure upon Vienna to keep out of Salisbury's schemes of forcing the Straits in November, and the insistence that, if there was to be any question of a revival of the old *entente à trois*, it must be on a much more sharply defined basis. Unless England was firmly com-mitted there was, they considered, a grave danger that *perfide Albion* would start a war in the Near East and then decide to withdraw, leaving Austria to face Russia alone. What Germany wanted, as the Emperor told Swaine at the end of December, was for England to take the initiative and force the Straits alone: this, they knew, would bring war with Russia and thus throw England back on to the Triple Alliance. All they had to do was wait: sooner or later this would occur. Hence the decision, in complete contrast to 1887, that, as Marschall told Lascelles,

Germany will not encourage her allies to seek an agreement with England unless a binding convention can be arrived at,

[1] Hamilton to Balfour, ibid.; Marder, ibid.; Goschen to Salisbury, 30 November, 2, 7, 22 December 1895, S.P.

since otherwise they fear England will not honour her obligations.[1]

In these circumstances the South African crisis arrived at a
disastrously opportune moment. Holstein and Hatzfeldt, rightly,
thought that German policy should be to maintain a complete
reserve; do nothing and wait until England came to them; as
Salisbury himself suggested, in time public opinion would forget
the Armenians and he would be able to resume the old policy of
supporting the *status quo*. But the Emperor would not let well
alone. Impulsive and erratic as usual he had been personally
irritated by a warning given by Malet in October that Germany
should keep out of Transvaal politics, and retaliated with threats
that if England did not join the Triple Alliance he would be
compelled to side with France and Russia. Annoyed by the end
of December that Salisbury would neither take the plunge alone
at the Straits—and thus bring on the Anglo-Russian war that
Germany was waiting for—nor support Italy in the Red Sea, he
now decided, when the Jameson Raid materialised, that this
should be exploited to put the pressure on England. The Transvaal seemed ideally suited to these ends. The traditional means
of squeezing England—Egypt—was dangerous at this moment
since, given its supreme importance, and his good relations with
France, Salisbury might turn round and negotiate with Paris.
This would defeat the whole object of German policy since the
one thing they depended on was the Egyptian issue keeping
London and Paris apart and thus making London willing to
support Rome. But the Transvaal possessed none of these dis-
advantages: it would hit England where it hurt yet it would not
matter to Germany, since it could easily be given up as the price
of an agreement. As Holstein later complained, 'I am fed up
with the whole of South Africa because we have nothing to gain
there under any circumstances.'[2]

The whole point then of the Kruger Telegram and Continental League, apart from the relief that it gave to the
Emperor's feelings, was to force Salisbury to give up his 'dangerous' policy in the Near East and reach a signed and sealed

[1] Lascelles to Salisbury 21 December 1895, S.P.; G.P., X, Nos. 2572,
2759; XI, No. 2800; H.P., III, Nos. 489, 490, 514, 515.
[2] H.P., III, pp. 551–4, No. 539; G.P., XI, No. 2759.

agreement with the Triple Alliance. It was this aspect that appealed to Hohenlohe. Alarmed, like Holstein and Hatzfeldt, by the Emperor's unnecessary vituperation in October, he had done what he could to tone down the effect of these remarks. Now, in January, however, he gave his adherence to the Kruger Telegram because, as he explained to Munster:

> When England has learnt through experience that the gap between the two great Continental groups is not unbridgeable, and that these groups, once agreed upon a definite point are strong enough to proceed to action over England's head, then, and only then, will England realise that independence leads to isolation and that isolation can be dangerous.

But the effect of this manoeuvre was altogether contrary to German expectations. The Continental League itself fell flat since its purpose was too transparently obvious: the French could see no point in helping Germany to force England into an alliance against them. In London, Salisbury himself was not particularly perturbed. If increasingly disturbed by what he later referred to as 'cette agitation croissante', he had long regarded William as unreliable: he had, he told Lascelles, been expecting something like this since the Emperor's gestures in October. But popular feeling, unprepared for this, and devoted to Jameson, was incensed and a wave of anti-German feeling now swept the Press. As *The Times* put it with studious moderation, if Great Britain were now to seek an alliance it 'would not be with Germany, but with the Powers which she, perhaps, regards not wholly without apprehension'.[1]

The South African crisis itself blew over with Salisbury's repudiation of Jameson and the failure of Russia and France to rise to the German bait, but the effects were to be far reaching. For most of the Cabinet, if not for Salisbury, this was their first direct experience of German hostility and the results were in proportion. Besides this the traditional dangers of France and Russia seemed relatively unimportant, as Hicks-Beach, the Chancellor of the Exchequer, agreed when Salisbury suggested an immediate increase in the naval estimates:

> What with present feeling in the United States and the

---

[1] *History of the Times*, III, p. 259; Salisbury to Lascelles 10 March 1896, S.P.; H.P., III, No. 532; G.P., XI, No. 2641; Langer, pp. 248-9.

Emperor telegraphing to Kruger, we have to think of other
things besides a Franco-Russian alliance against us.

By the spring the Russian Ambassador at London, de Staal, was
reporting both Chamberlain and Balfour as strongly pro-
Russian, whilst Courcel, with an agreement on Siam just signed,
thought the moment had even arrived for an Anglo-French
understanding over Egypt: he did not see how, in view of public
feeling in London, Anglo-German relations could ever be the
same again. The position was well summarised by Hamilton,
writing in the New Year to Balfour, who was currently engaged
in persuading Salisbury that there had to be changes in foreign
policy:

> I have great sympathy for Salisbury and his practice of holding
> few and far Cabinets enhances his difficulties as he nurses a
> policy until the time comes for expression in action and he then
> finds his cabinet against him and has to retrace his steps. This
> for a strong and proud man must be very unpleasant. . . . The
> German alliance and safeguarding of Constantinople are two
> objects for which he has persistently worked during his last ten
> years. He now appreciates fully to what it has led and is leading.
>
> We cannot keep Russia out of Constantinople but our futile
> efforts have consolidated friendship between Russia and France
> and brought us kicks from Germany and from other nations.
> We must alter our action, but we have been so blind in the past
> that a mere recital of our past policy is a heavy indictment of
> the policy pursued. A memo written by you and sent to the
> Cabinet cannot fail, however judiciously worded, to . . . put
> Salisbury in the dock before his own Cabinet.[1]

The effects of this were immediately visible in February 1896
when Goluchowski at last raised the question of a revision of the
Mediterranean Agreements. With the brief exception of his
initiative on 11 November, Goluchowski had allowed Austrian
policy towards England to be dictated from Berlin. Even in
January 1896, after the Kruger Telegram, echoing almost word
for word German views, he told Crispi that before negotiating
with England they must wait for the outbreak of the expected
Anglo-Russian war: 'then it will be possible to make a precise

[1] Hamilton to Balfour 12 January 1896, Add. MSS. 49778; Hicks-
Beach to Salisbury 5 January 1896, P.C.C., 33; de Staal, II, p. 309; Hargreaves, *Entente Manquée* in C.H.J., 1953, pp. 83–84.

and binding agreement'. But if Vienna were quite happy with the situation, this was far from being the case in Rome. By the end of 1895 the Italian position in Abyssinia was becoming desperate. Partly as a result of some limited aid from Russia and France, Menelik was now in a position to issue an open challenge and on 7 December defeated an Italian column at Amba-Alagi. For reasons of internal politics it was essential to get a victory by the spring but, due to logistical difficulties, the only way to achieve this was by using Zeila and thus take Menelik in the flank. Hence the desperate need for a general understanding with England, whatever Berlin might say, and the series of offers of assistance to England at Constantinople: if, as Blanc and Crispi suspected, the current Anglo-Russian co-operation at Constantinople were extended to the Red Sea, then Italy would be ruined. Doubting strongly the German thesis of the inevitability of an Anglo-Russian war which would force England to come to the Triple Alliance, they wanted negotiations with London to begin at once. But since all their attempts to move Vienna in December had failed, they were forced to attempt a separate understanding. Their major difficulty was that in asking Salisbury for either cession or access to Zeila they were in effect asking him to break a long-standing agreement with France, at a time when good relations with France were extremely important to him. Moreover, Italy had nothing to offer in exchange. Italian aid in the Mediterranean, which was readily forthcoming, was of no use to Salisbury unless it could bring Austrian too; which it could not. Yet, in the delicate state of affairs at Constantinople, and with an agreement on Siam all but signed, it would be madness to risk alienating France. Hence the only concessions which Salisbury would make over Zeila were so hedged around with conditions as to be almost useless, a state of affairs which played a considerable part in the production of the Kruger Telegram.[1]

But however much Blanc, Crispi's Foreign Minister, might rage at British perfidy—'les Anglais ont la tête dans un sac, ils ne voient rien'—and welcome the Continental League as a means of pressure on London, this in fact solved none of Italy's

[1] Pasetti to Goluchowski 13, 25 January 1896, S.A.W., Geheimakten XXV, Karton Rot, 463.5A–E, 7C; Hargreaves, pp. 77–78; Walters, *Lord Salisbury's Refusal* . . . in *Slavonic Review*, December 1950, pp. 271 et. seq.

problems. As it became clear that the German action, far from impressing London, had merely made relations between England and Germany worse, even Blanc now began to doubt their judgment. As he complained to Goluchowski:

> The Berlin Cabinet which, as soon as the Eastern Question is raised, says it is only secondarily concerned, chooses to treat as of first importance a colonial question which concerns Germany much less than the East, and her allies not at all.

Crispi, who had never shared Blanc's optimism anyway, was now seriously alarmed since it was his conviction that the Kruger Telegram indicated that the intention of Berlin was to cut adrift from England and re-create the old *Dreikaiserbund*. This in itself would be ruinous for Italian interests in the Mediterranean and the Red Sea, in view of the current Russian concern with Abyssinia, but, Crispi thought, worse would follow: to protect herself England would then retaliate with an Anglo-Russian-French partition of the Ottoman Empire. Hence, in the Italian view, whatever Berlin might say, it was essential to open negotiations at London immediately: if Salisbury could be pinned down to a firm alliance so much the better, but, if not, it was still essential to at least renew the existing agreements for the preservation of the *status quo*; if only to prevent him doing a deal with Russia. Since Crispi coupled his insistence on negotiations with England with the demand that otherwise Italy would make the renewal of the Triple Alliance dependent upon increased support from his German allies in both the Mediterranean and the Red Sea, Goluchowski was at last stirred into action.[1]

Deym's exploratory interview on 23 January went reasonably well. Salisbury explained that Hohenlohe's demand that England should join the Triple Alliance was unreasonable: it was a far greater obligation than he could undertake, especially in view of present opinion towards Germany: Parliament would reject such a course out of hand. But this did not apply to the Mediterranean understanding since here strong British interests were involved and the British public would always fight any power who threatened these. This seemed encouraging to Deym and he now took up Goluchowski's specific question: would the

[1] Pasetti to Goluchowski 13 January, 5A–E; 25 January, 7A–G, 7C, ibid.; Crispi, *Questioni Internazionali*, pp. 280–1, 286–7.

Cabinet bind themselves to maintain Constantinople and would they modify the 1887 agreement to that effect? Here the rift at once appeared. Salisbury explained the experts views on forcing the Straits and, while pointing out that he personally did not believe the experts, admitted regretfully that the Cabinet did. Possibly a guarantee of 20,000 Austrian troops to attack the landward side might influence them, but he was uncertain. Moreover,

> not to be forgotten was public opinion in England, which was very bitter towards Turkey and it was very questionable if the country would undertake a war on her behalf.

But he would re-read the 1887 agreements and see what could be done.

Salisbury saw Deym again on 4 February after he had consulted Balfour. The result was conclusive. Public opinion, according to the Leader of the House, was such that any agreement to defend Turkey would certainly be repudiated and, whilst it was possible that opinion might swing if Russia seized Constantinople, this could not be relied upon. He could give no binding commitment because he would not risk misleading the Austrian Government; however he would renew, if they wished, the 1887 agreement:

> Je vous l'avouerai franchement. C'est que cet accord ne m'engage pas à grand chose, car il ne nous oblige pas à faire la guerre.

As far as Goluchowski was concerned this was the end of the policy of collaboration with England. Never settling very great hopes of success on these negotiations, which he had only been pushed into by Crispi, he now simply accepted the German view that half a loaf was worse than none, a view agreed at a meeting with Hohenlohe in March. Crispi might rage at this and threaten Italian exit from the alliance but, at least until Adua, Hohenlohe was indifferent.[1]

Clearly therefore, the responsibility for the breakdown of the association of England with the Triple Alliance in the Mediterranean, lay in Berlin and Vienna, not in London. Salisbury,

---

[1] Deym to Goluchowski 23 January, 6 February, 7A–F, 1896, ihid.; B.D., VIII, pp. 4–5; Walters, pp. 276–9; G.P., XI, No. 2767.

although admitting his inability to satisfy Goluchowski's requests that the understanding be converted into an alliance, still did his best to give Vienna and Berlin confidence in British policy. To Deym he had emphasised that, even if they could not come to an agreement, there was a complete identity of interest with Austria in the Near East; whilst to Berlin he was quite categorical that there had been no change in the British attitude:

> We certainly wish to be good friends with Germany: as we were in 1892. That is to say we wish to lean to the Triple Alliance without belonging to it. But in 1892, as now, we kept free from any engagements to go to war in any contingency whatever. . . . Whether this attitude is reasonable or not it is the attitude we maintained from 1886–1892. If the German Emperor is dissatisfied with us now why was he satisfied with us then? There is no change.

His purpose in this was quite simple. The Cabinet itself was divided on foreign policy: some, particularly the more vocal were for abandoning traditional policy completely after the Kruger Telegram and seeking an understanding with Russia. But Salisbury himself did not share this view and, although he could not induce his colleagues to make any commitments to the Triple Alliance, he got sufficient support, particularly from Goschen, to avoid any radical departures at this stage. This was made clear in a letter to the Queen on 19 February 1896, summarising the Cabinet's discussion of the reply that should be given to Goluchowski's enquiries:

> Mr. Chamberlain was of the opinion that at the point where we were now our antagonism to Russia was a mistake and that we should occupy a stronger position in Europe as the friend of Russia than as the friend of the Triple Alliance. This view was not generally shared by the Cabinet but opinions were much divided. Generally it was agreed that we should never be allowed by the people of this country to go to war again on behalf of Turkey, though we might do so in defence of the Straits to prevent them from being appropriated by Russia. The opinion was generally expressed that feeling in this country even on the Tory side was much more favourable to Russia and much more adverse to the Turks than it used to be. Lord Salisbury expressed himself strongly against any policy that would cut Austria adrift. It would reconstitute the Drei

Kaiser Bundnis, a state of affairs which must be injurious to this country.[1]

But the problem, in the face of public opinion and the views of his colleagues, was just how to give Vienna and Berlin this renewed confidence in British policy. The opportunity arose almost immediately in March 1896 with the Italian defeat by Menelik at Adua on 1 March. This brought the complete collapse of Crispi's colonial policy and serious rioting in Milan and Rome which the republican groups began to exploit. In turn this led Vienna and Berlin to fear that, unless immediate support were given, Italy, as the French Press was already predicting, would leave the alliance. Hence the Emperor's dramatic appeal to Lascelles on 3 March for a gesture of solidarity on England's part, long before the Italian Government asked for any assistance at all. This appeal Salisbury was quick to exploit. On 4 March he saw Hatzfeldt, reassured him of England's good intentions and her desire to be on good terms with the alliance, ascribing all the difficulties in the recent negotiations with Deym to his colleagues and the strength of public opinion. On 12 March he ordered the advance to Dongola. It was not that this was of much use to the Italians in Africa—as they quickly pointed out—but it was a gesture, a clear enough indication, as Salisbury assured Hatzfeldt, of the British desire to continue to work with the Triple Alliance. Happily now, it seemed, the period of British collaboration with France and Russia, which had been so evident in 1895, was over, and the danger of an Egyptian settlement following that on Siam—a possibility which Hatzfeldt at least had taken seriously after the failure of the Continental League—excluded. As, instead, there was increasing friction between England, France and Russia over Salisbury's application to the *Caisse* for the costs of the advance into the Sudan, Berlin could rejoice once more and, characteristically, the Emperor now congratulated himself on the success of his *coup*. He conveniently forgot that it was his own action which had caused most of the trouble in the first place.[2]

[1] Salisbury to the Queen 19 February 1896, S.P.; Salisbury to Lascelles 10 March 1896, S.P. Hatzfeldt was convinced that Salisbury wished to retain the old links with Berlin: to Holstein 15 March 1896, H.P., III, No. 532.

[2] G.P., XI, Nos. 2673, 2779, 2694, 2681–3, 2713; H.P., III, Nos. 531, 534.

In point of fact this danger was largely imaginary. Whatever Hatzfeldt may have thought or Crispi feared, there is no reason to suppose that Salisbury ever contemplated a general settlement with France at this stage. Courcel certainly hoped that something might be accomplished in this direction after the Kruger Telegram, but this was to misread its effects on Salisbury, judging only from public opinion. In 1896, as in 1887, what Salisbury wanted primarily was still to control Russia at the Straits and, as Courcel himself recognised, France had little influence over Russia in this respect. If, as seemed obvious, Germany was fast moving towards support for Russia and away from her old alignment with England, it seemed only common sense to Salisbury to check this by reinsurance with the Triple Alliance. Hence, as far as Salisbury was concerned, the decision to order the advance to Dongola presented no problem, there was no question of regarding a settlement with France as an alternative, especially now that Egypt was becoming the second line of defence in the Mediterranean.[1]

In the spring of 1896 then the situation was still fluid. The Mediterranean Agreements had not been turned into the alliance as Berlin and Vienna required, nor had they been simply renewed as Salisbury wanted. The Kruger Telegram had not produced the Continental League that Berlin had hoped for, but equally it had not led to the English understanding with France that Hatzfeldt feared. Instead the Italian disaster at Adua had been used both by Berlin and London as a means to a *rapprochement* between England and the Triple Alliance, which at least patched up the differences for the moment and enabled Italy, in June, to renew her alliance with the German powers for a fourth term. The importance of England in this respect was clearly demonstrated by Rudinì, who replaced Crispi in March, since he insisted on making a public declaration that the alliance was only possible as long as it was compatible with good relations with London.[2] With British troops advancing in the Sudan this seemed safe enough, but a renewed massacre of the

[1] Hargreaves, pp. 85–90; Goschen told Deym that the main reason he supported the Dongola move was in order to re-create the old relationship with the Triple Alliance: to Goluchowski 24 April 1896, S.A.W., VIII, 118.-19A–B.

[2] Pribram, II, pp. 112–13; D.D.I., 1, No. 60.

Armenians in August swiftly changed the position and, this time, finally put an end to the understanding with England in the Mediterranean.

Salisbury's hopes, as expressed to Deym and Hatzfeldt in March, that gradually public opinion would forget the Armenians and permit the restoration of the old understanding, obviously depended upon the Eastern Question remaining dormant. But a renewal in August 1896 of the massacres of 1895 brought up again all the old problems, obliged Salisbury to think again of forcing the Straits, and thus brought out once more the complete divergence of British and Austrian policy. Goluchowski, it seems, had regarded the old alliance as dead since March, despite Salisbury's attempts to keep it alive: certainly in August he made it quite clear that there was no possibility of further co-operation, that as things were he had more in common with Russia than with England. By August this was probably true, as Salisbury discovered when he himself tried to get Russian agreement for action at the Straits; they, like Austria, much preferred the *status quo*. In this situation, rejected by Russia and Austria alike, who both preferred to leave the Armenians to their fate, Salisbury now resigned himself to the inevitable:

> The three Emperors have agreed to maintain the status quo of the Turkish territory. I am convinced that any occupation of the territory by us would lead to war with some of them. Rosebery I see takes the same view. That course may, I think, be put aside.

This had important consequences. Now more than ever it was clearly impossible to consider supporting Turkey and the policy of defending the Straits had to be finally abandoned. For the present, as Salisbury told the Ambassador in Vienna in January 1897, there was no need to make this public knowledge; but obviously now England had to fall back on the second line of defence suggested by the N.I.D. in November 1895, 'the absolute and permanent occupation of Egypt'.[1]

[1] Marder, p. 248; Salisbury to Hicks-Beach 5 October 1896, P.C.C., 66; Salisbury to Rumbold 20 January 1897, B.B., IX (1) p. 775–6; Walters, *Austro-Russian relations under Goluchowski*, 1895—1908, in *Slavonic Review*, 1952–3, pp. 229–31.

It was this change, really, which ended the one bond of common interest between England and Germany and determined the failure of the various attempts at an Anglo-German alliance. Berlin insisted that the only alliance she would admit was what she had been after since 1890: British adherence to the Triple Alliance. From the German point of view this was understandable enough: only British cement would hold Italy who, by 1897, was moving fast towards a settlement with France. But from the British viewpoint by 1897 this was a pointless proposition. The whole object of the policy pursued from 1887 until 1896 had been to keep Italy in the alliance in order that she could be used to obtain the assistance of the German powers at Constantinople. But by 1897 this was invalid. British policy could no longer support Turkey; Germany and Austria preferred an understanding with Russia. In these circumstances what possible point could there be in continuing to support Italy? As the D.M.I. bluntly expressed the position in October 1896:

> Italy by herself is but a broken reed to lean upon, but as a link to bind England to a powerful confederation she is worthy of confronting risks and entering into engagements. The policy of a guarantee, as far as merely ensuring the support of Italy alone . . . presents but trivial attractions.[1]

That British policy was changing was equally evident to Rome. Though not certain of the cause of this swing the leading Italian diplomats were convinced, by the autumn of 1896, that the old policy of association with the Triple Alliance in the Mediterranean was waning and that it would probably be replaced by a *rapprochement* with France and Russia. Recognition of this fact played an important part in the changes that now occurred in Italian policy, since it was essential that Italy should reach agreement with France before England did: otherwise France would have no reason to bother to make concessions. As a result negotiations over Tunis were rapidly brought to a successful conclusion and, by 1902, a similar agreement over Tripoli and Morocco followed, a by-product of which was a virtual declaration of neutrality by Italy in the event of a Franco-German war. The main reason that Italy did not leave

[1] Marder, pp. 576–80.

the alliance was that, as the French pointed out, she was better protected against her allies by remaining inside it.[1]

The responsibility for this state of affairs rested largely with Bismarck's successors. The great thing to be said for Bismarck's policy was that it worked. His treaty with Russia may have been contrary to his understanding with England or to the spirit of his commitments to Austria, but at least he managed to keep them all happy. It may well be, as his advances of January 1889 suggest, that he too would have preferred the simplicity of a military alliance with England. But he was sufficient of a realist, when this was unattainable, to appreciate that half a cake was better than none. Undoubtedly the intentions of his successors were honourable and, especially under Caprivi, they were mainly directed towards an even closer connection with England. But the mistake they made was to allow their obsession with a clean-cut solution to dominate their policy since, in practice, the ultimatum that either England joined the alliance or was pushed into isolation, inevitably meant that the latter course followed: and, by destroying the Mediterranean *entente*, Berlin also destroyed the Triple Alliance. This would have made sense if it could have been replaced by Salisbury's bugbear, the alliance of the Three Emperors. But, after the Franco-Russian alliance, this proved impossible, as Hohenlohe reluctantly recognised by March 1896.[2] There was very little left now that Germany could do except wait for the Anglo-Russian or Anglo-French war, since there was now no hope otherwise of an English alliance on the terms Germany needed. Once England had lost interest in the Straits she had lost interest in the Triple Alliance, as Salisbury pointed out in his last contribution to foreign policy, the memorandum against a German alliance of 29 May 1901 :

The liability of having to defend the German and Austrian frontiers against Russia is heavier than that of having to defend the British Isles against France.[3]

During these ten years it is no exaggeration to say that British

---

[1] D.D.I., 1, Nos. 244, 252, 163; Serra, 25–27, 44.
[2] G.P., XI, No. 2676.
[1] Memorandum by Salisbury in B.D., II, No. 86.

foreign policy had been almost entirely determined by Mediterranean problems. Of these, still in 1896, by far the most important was the traditional interest in the prevention of Russian control of the Straits. As long as this could be prevented Egypt, though important, was a secondary interest: only with the realisation, reluctantly accepted by Salisbury, that the traditional policy was no longer possible, did Egypt move up into first place as the key now to British Mediterranean policy and communication with India. This explains a lot. As long as the major object of British foreign policy was to keep Russia out of Constantinople then an alliance of some sort with the German powers was essential: as Salisbury had said in 1887 this was as close to an alliance as England could get. But this did not necessarily entail bad relations with France: on the contrary, though it was obvious by 1887 that France would never fight Russia, it was equally clear that she had no more desire than England to see Russian control of Constantinople. Hence, until 1896, the Egyptian question was kept as quiet as possible to avoid exacerbating relations with France and the anti-French aspects of the Mediterranean Agreements, largely of Italian manufacture, toned down to the minimum.

It is true of course that there were, particularly under Rosebery, variations on this theme from time to time; it is arguable that already by 1894 serious attempts were being made at a settlement with Russia. But these do not detract from the accuracy of the general picture that, until forced to do so by the change in German policy and in British public opinion, Salisbury still clung to the old policy of defence of the Straits in concert with the Triple Alliance. But the change, when it came, in 1896, had momentous consequences. Sticking in Egypt and treating the Straits as negotiable meant that the Austrian alliance was no longer of any importance to England: the enemy was now France, not Russia, and France could always be handled without the assistance of the Triple Alliance.

BIBLIOGRAPHY

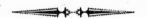

The following abbreviations have been made:

I. MANUSCRIPTS

A.M.E.   Archivio Ministero dell'Estero, Rome
A.S.C.   Archivio di Stato Centrale, Rome
B.P.   Balfour Papers, British Museum Add. MSS
F.O.   Foreign Office Correspondence, Public Record Office
K.P.   Kimberley Papers, Public Record Office
M.R.R.   Museo del Risorgimento, Rome
P.C.C.   Hicks-Beach Papers, Williamstrip Park, Gloucester
S.A.W.   Haus, Hof-und Staatsarchiv, Vienna
S.P.   Salisbury Papers, Christchurch Library, Oxford

II. PRINTED MATERIAL

A.P.   *Atti Parlamentari, Deputati*
B.D.   *British Documents on the Origin of the War*, ed. Gooch and Temperley, London, 1927 ff.
D.D.F.   *Documents Diplomatiques Francais, lre série*, Paris, 1929 ff.
D.D.I.   *Documenti Diplomatici Italiani 3a seria*, Rome, 1950 ff.
G.P.   *Die Grosse Politik der Europäischen Kabinette*, ed. Lipsius, Bartholdy and Thimme, Berlin, 1922–7
H.P.   *Holstein Papers, Vol. III. Correspondence*, ed. Rich and Fisher, London, 1960

III. MEMOIRS, BIOGRAPHIES, ETC.

Billot, *La France et l'Italie, 1881–99*, Paris, 1905
Buckle (ed), *Letters of Queen Victoria, IIIrd series*, London, 1930
Cecil, *Life of Robert Marquis of Salisbury*, Vol. IV, London, 1932
Chiala, *Pagine di storia contemporanea*, Turin, 1898
Crispi, *Politica estera*, Milan, 1913
—— *Questioni Internazionali*, Milan, 1913
—— *La prima guerra d'Africa*, Milan, 1914
Farini, *Diario, 1891–5* (ed. Morelli), Milan, 1942
Gorrini, *Tunisi e Biserta. Memorie storiche di Giacomo Gorrini*, Milan, 1940

Hamilton, *Parliamentary Reminiscences and Reflections*, London, 1922
Luzzatti, *Memorie*, Bologna, 1935
Stillman, *Francesco Crispi*, London, 1899

IV. SECONDARY STUDIES

Anon. *History of the Times*, Vol. III, London, 1948
Bayer, *England und der neue Kurs 1890–95*, Tubingen, 1955
Chabod, *Storia della politica estera italiana 1870–1896*, Bari, 1951
Grenville, *Goluchowski, Salisbury, and the Mediterranean Agreements* in *Slavonic Review 1958*
Hargreaves, *Entente Manquée* in *Cambridge Historical Journal*, 1953
Hermann, *Zweibund, Dreibund, England*, Stuttgart, 1929
Israel, *England und der Orientalische Dreibund*, Stuttgart, 1937
James, *Rosebery*, London, 1963
Langer, *The Franco–Russian Alliance*, Cambridge, Mass., 1929
—— *European Alliances and Alignments*, New York, 1950
—— *The Diplomacy of Imperialism*, New York, 1950
Marder, *The Anatomy of British Sea Power*, London, 1942
Medlicott, *The Mediterranean Agreements of 1887* in *Slavonic Review*, 1926
Meyendorff, *Correspondence diplomatique de M. de Staal*, Paris, 1929
Penson, *The New Course in British Foreign Policy 1892–1907* in *T.R.H.S.*, Vol. XXV
Pribram, *The Secret Treaties of Austria–Hungary*, Cambridge, Mass., 1921
Robinson and Gallacher, *Africa and the Victorians*, London, 1961
Roemer, *England und die europäischen Machte im Jahre 1887*, Aarau, 1957
Salvatorelli, *La Triplice Alleanza*, Milan, 1939
Salvemini, *La politica estera di Francesco Crispi*, Florence, 1919
—— *La politica estera dell'Italia 1871–1914*, Florence, 1944
Serra, *L'intesa mediterranean del 1903*, Milan, 1956
Shibeika, *British Policy in the Sudan 1882–1902*, London, 1952
Smith, *The Embassy of Sir William White at Constantinople 1886–1892*, Oxford, 1957
Temperley and Penson, *The Foundations of British Foreign Policy 1792–1902*, London, 1938
Volpe, *L'Italia moderna*, Vol. I, Florence, 1942
Walters, *Lord Salisbury's refusal to revise and renew the Mediterranean Agreements* in *Slavonic Review*, 1950–51
—— *Austro–Russian relations under Goluchowski 1895–1908* in *Slavonic Review*, 1952–3
Zaghi, *P. S. Mancini, L'Africa e il problema del Mediterraneo 1884–5*, Rome, 1955

INDEX

Abyssinia, 61; *see also* Zeila
Armenian question, 99–105, 115

Balfour, Arthur James, 53, 87, 104, 108, 111
Beresford, Admiral Lord Charles, 43, 86
Bismark, Prince Otto von, and policy in Bulgaria (1886), 6; advises Italy to seek British alliance (1886), 12; object in this, 15–16; supports *entente à trois*, 21; attitude to war (1888), 27, 45–46; proposes Anglo-German alliance (1889) 45–46, 54, 58; comparison with successors, 73, 117
Bizerta, 65–67; *see also* Tunis, Tripoli
Blanc, Baron Alberto, 20–21, 109–10
Boulanger, General, 19, 32
Brin, Admiral, 34, 77, 90, 93
Bulgaria, 2, 6, 20, 22, 26

Caprivi, General Georg von, and 'New Course', 58–59; and Bizerta (1890), 66; welcomes appointment of Rosebery, 92; rejects Rosebery's approaches (1894), 94–96
Chamberlain, Joseph, 3, 52, 89, 104, 108, 112

Churchill, Lord Randolph, 4–5, 18
Constantinople, object of defence of, Chapter I *passim*, 55–56; Rosebery offers to defend, 95; defence of abandoned by Salisbury, 116–18; *see also* Armenian question
Crispi, Francesco, initiates *entente à trois* (1887), 20–21, 25; character and outlook upon foreign policy, 29–31; and France, 27–29, 31–33; and Austria, 33, 39; seeks naval alliance with Britain, 35–36, 39, 50–51, 81–82; and Tunis, 49; and Sudan (1890), 61–64; and Tripoli (1890), 65; and Ottoman Empire, 68–69; and military convention with Germany, 27, 74; seeks alliance with Britain (1894), 97; and Armenian question, 100–2; and renewel of *entente à trois*, 109–10

Dilke, Sir Charles, 1
Drummond-Wolff, Sir Henry, 18–20

Egypt, 2–3, 13–14, 56–57, 71–72, 118; *see also* Kassala, Sudan

121

INDEX